MASTER
LEADERS
The Art of Influence

"Those who refuse their calling to lead, will lose
their power to lead." —JWW & JWP

By

James W. White & James W. Pickens

"There are too many so-called leaders who want to tear down something but are unwilling to build that something up."—JWW & JWP

"As in life, master leaders are exceptional individuals who celebrate victories and at times have to suffer for their passions."—JWW & JWP

ISBN: 0615570933
ISBN 13: 9780615570938

MASTER —————

LEADERS

The Art of Influence

DEDICATION

We would like to thank some wonderful people whose love and encouragement made this book possible. Additionally, we'd like to thank all the great leaders from around the United States who contributed to this work.

Jim White – *Dedicated to my father, who taught me the difference between fault and responsibility, to my mother whose love and suggestion prompted this book, and to my amazing wife and children who stand faithfully beside me throughout all of my endeavors.*

Jim Pickens - *Dedicated to Lindsey Janell Pickens and Barbara D. Johnson*

CONTENTS

Author's Note

There is not a successful corporation in the world that does not have a leader who is aggressive, devoted, caring, and truly passionate about success at its helm. Employees need and want a director who understands them, works by their side, and teaches and motivates them to be the very best they can be. This book is about brave men and women who are willing to sacrifice their time and energy for the good of others while developing an incredibly strong work environment. Master leaders become exceptional executives because they find, at some point in their lives, a cause so great and profound that they are willing to give everything they have to promote and ensure its survival. This explanation on what makes leaders special is not complex. Every leader who has identified his or her cause will use their personality, skills of persuasion, and influence to allow all those around them to see and understand the same vision. Of course, there are people with bad and dark intentions who become leaders by default but tend to self-destruct and/or their game is discovered and destroyed.

Good and decent leaders last a lifetime because they are a catalyst for hope and aspiration. They lead charismatically and are successful because they involve everyone in their world to participate and evoke a feeling of importance and necessity.

This work is devoted to the powerful men and women who daily put their personal reputation and courage on the line for their employees. Gifted people, who truly make other people feel good about themselves. The master leader is not a superhero or saint, but a single individual who is daring enough to take risks, ask questions, seek advice, and fight for his or her convictions. The leader is respected because he keeps his word, treats employees as equals, and never forgets where he came from.

We wish you the very best. God bless you.

Your friends,
James W. White and James W. Pickens

INTRODUCTION

Jesus said, "Anyone who puts their hands to the plow and looks backwards is not worthy of my kingdom." This simple but very powerful statement is one of the key secrets to leadership success. This inspiring lesson has been adopted, perfected and kept close to the heart of countless international master leaders. Now, of course, leaders will reflect and study the past so future mistakes are avoided, but they'll never dwell on the past or totally rely on it for progress or prosperity. Master leaders are constantly surveying the ever-changing horizon, believing in tomorrow with its endless possibilities, and always maintaining a positive and unafraid attitude while they attempt the impossible. Leaders are motivated and guided by their dreams and dedication yet aware of those who desire to derail or sabotage their good intentions. Leaders don't lose or let the people around them lose. They bring everyone they come in contact with into a sphere of energy. A sphere that generates a Can Do spirit packed with goodness and determination. Master leaders know the ancient truth, "If you want to be great, you must make the people around you greater."

Reader, the information in this leadership book is based on proven management and executive facts and procedures that, when faithfully practiced, will get any organization or sales team performing at their very best. This volume was written strictly to help you become a master leader—a courageous goal that all salespeople, managers, sales directors, and executives should try in every honest way to achieve. This book will in fact transform any determined and hardworking person into a highly successful leader. A person who takes total control over any situation or challenge and always delivers victory. A victory that, when examined, encompasses all, encourages all, and honors all. Now, what exactly is a master leader? For starters, it's a very brave and bold person who, by example, has gained the complete respect of everyone in the firm. In addition, it is someone who can get any business organization or company to produce optimally under all kinds of conditions, situations, or dilemmas.

On the book market today, there are many publications that portray corporate executives, general leaders, or directors of sales in a simple monolithic prototype. This manual is different. Leaders vary in outlooks and expressions. We, the authors, think whatever one's personality, there is a special type of leader he or she can identify with. Reader, by coupling your drive to succeed with the unique strategies, lessons, and tips presented here, you will experience repeated success as a master leader. This is a fascinating and fulfilling position where the sky is truly the limit and people are your best natural resource.

To become a master leader, you must begin now and with absolute resolve. The whole world is waiting for a person who can share wisdom, inspire, and comfort. Keep in mind, if you don't become all you think you can be, millions of people will be led by others who don't have your heart, knowledge, daring, and, most important, love. If not you, then who, we ask? Remember this truth: leaders are made and not born. Again, anyone can become a leader if they find a purpose in their life they are willing to give all for. Let this book help guide you into the command centers of international corporations where you can take absolute control as a self-made sovereign! A leader who is fair, truthful, and clothed in compassion.

....

"The true master leader is a warrior with a heart."

J. L. MELLON, PITTSBURGH, PA

....

1.

The Master Leader Described

CHAPTER 1

THE MASTER LEADER

A master leader is a person who not only can influence and lead others by example, but one who also shows great courage, love, and conviction when working with his or her fellow colleagues. He or she is a true professional no matter the time, place, or situation.

"The more I know, the more I know I know nothing."

JOHN HUNT, DALLAS, TX

1. THE DIFFERENT TYPES OF MASTER LEADERS

As stated before, there are many management books in stores today that have their own interpretation of what a successful corporate executive or general manager should be. There are books and articles written on how he or she should act, what they should study, how they should dress, when they should exhibit political correctness, or use technical jargon, and how they should establish their position through titles, problem solving, and trying to negotiate everything.

These books have their good points, of course, but nearly all of them put the subject of leadership under such a high-powered microscope that readers historically find them ineffective and forgettable.

Lost in the tangle of high tech language and theories, programs, and lists of rules is the master leader's professional and fundamental purpose: influencing customers, office staff, and salespeople to understand, appreciate, and value the leader's company and product while also leading, motivating, and educating the sales and office teams to produce and facilitate the highest volume of transactions they are physically and mentally capable of achieving.

Those texts that try to create and mass-produce step-in company programs that offer cheering employee templates are missing a very important point. People are egotistically different. Master leaders know for a fact that salespeople, support staff, and general managers do not come in perfectly organized and stereotyped molds. Each and every person who works with the leader is a very novel and independent individual. Now, to direct such people, a leader might well use unorthodox and sometimes unique methods at times. Yet they will also be earning respect and admiration from company executives at the same time. Why? It's simple: They treated everyone justly. They showed everyone courtesy, and let them develop their talents to the fullest through encouragement, appreciation, and truthfulness. Again, while true leaders conquer their objectives in many different, imaginative, and fascinating ways, they all have the common ability to give their sales and office people a feeling of sincerity and warmth. It may sound too simple or overly naïve, but when all the technical management terminology and in-vogue ideas are taken away, the only words that correctly describe the very foundation of a master leader's influencing skills and overall day-to-day attitude are "respect, understanding, and love."

Each and every master has his own idiosyncrasies and his or her own way of doing things. But when all is said and done, the successful and confident projection of the leader's belief in others, trying to understand others, and attentiveness to others will always be the special keys towards winning results and creating and a powerful corporation. Everyone knows and understands athletic coaches and their many different styles of coaching. If one visualizes the master leader as a professional coach with their sales team, support group, and office staff making up the team, the following general descriptions of leaders will then be more easily recognized, understood, and appreciated.

"The opportunities I've missed...by not listening to everyone who had an idea or suggestion."

SHARON BROCHETTE, BENTONVILLE, AR

The Wall Street Master Leader

This is the master leader who looks like he just stepped out of a fashion magazine. With his courtesy and perfect manners, he gets along with everyone, from the president of a large international corporation to the greenest rookie in a small sales company. The Wall Street leader is a perfect gentleman. He reads, studies, and listens to all the information he can find pertaining to people, sales, management, and leadership. You can put him in New York City or in Round Rock, Nevada, and he'll succeed in one way or another every single time. He knows what he is doing and has that "do or die" determination to achieve his goals.

At times, especially during an important business conversation, he can be downright intimidating. His business expertise, prowess, and command of all the relevant company and sales facts and figures can make a less-informed colleague feel uncomfortable. At no time, however, will this leader purposefully throw his expertise around to boost his own ego or to put someone else down.

While the Wall Street leader takes his job and responsibilities very seriously, he is not too distant to listen and empathize with his office and sales staff, taking into consideration their personal goals and problems. This leader has his head on straight. He successfully leads his men and women by not only knowing his company's business thoroughly, but also by looking the part of a prosperous businessman. His impeccable grooming and wardrobe reflect his brand of leadership and professionalism. He is as likely to compliment one of his fellow workers for a smart new suit as he is to applaud a sterling office or sales performance. While few people in the company feel really close to this kind of leader, everyone admires and respects him: he does, after all is said and done, get positive results.

....

"If opportunity doesn't knock, build your own door?"

UNKNOWN

....

The Good Old Boy Master Leader

If the Wall Street leader is never seen without his well-tailored suit, the Good Old Boy leader's sport jacket is often slung over a shoulder or on the back of the chair. Just as the name implies, everyone likes this type of master leader, from the corporation's owners to the janitors who maintain it. They feel close to him because he is always polite, has time to listen to others, and genuinely understands.

The Good Old Boy leader has a pure and sincere country air about him. In fact, he's a lot like an old-time, down-home philosopher in the way he handles different sales and office management situations. For example, when someone in his company has a problem, the Good Old Boy is the first person to console and take the time to listen. This kind of leader calms the troubled employee and eases any emotional burden by analyzing the problem himself. In fact, this involved leader is so close to his employees he actually treats problems as if they were his own.

This leader knows the in's and out's of a professional office as well as the Wall Street leader, but he never seems to use his knowledge as a badge. His strong point is intimately knowing all of his employees and how best to work with them. The Good Old Boy honestly cares about his people and treats them like family, and his staff returns his affection with record-breaking productivity.

"If I don't understand my people, then I don't understand anything."

SCOTT ANDERSON, PHOENIX, AZ

The Fear and Intimidation Master Leader

This leader has lightning in their eyes and thunder in their voices. Maybe that's why the office sees no storm clouds and feels no ripples on the high seas of office operations. At times employees feel like they've got Captain Ahab at the helm. Some will grumble and even threaten to desert, but the crew that stays on has an abiding respect for this domineering leader and a burning desire to perform at their best.

True, the Fear and Intimidation leader can be as rough and demanding as a marine drill sergeant, but they're doing the job professionally, financially benefiting the company and it's office staff. This no-holds-barred leader exhibits a heart of cold steel but, in reality, they have a heart of gold for all who are loyal. They'll do anything within their power to help out one an employee who gets in trouble, but that employee had better be ready for a good old dressing down when the problem is cleared up.

This masterful leader can control and motivate hundreds of people at one time. They run the staff meetings like a commander in a war room. Then again, they can take on one individual and give him or her all the attention and straightening out needed to get everything back on a sound, productive business track.

This bold leader wants a lean and mean sales force and staff and won't hesitate to give a slacker his or her discharge. Any firing will usually be discreet, without a stormy public scene. While this leader can be brutal at times, they always behave like a professional military officer. For example, at an office meeting, they'll explain that a missing colleague no longer maintains a fruitful relationship with the firm.

Somehow this icy euphemism is far more effective than a middle manager's loud ranting why so-and-so was fired. Instead of conspiratorial grumbling and sympathy resignations, the whole staff will tend to rally around their leader with loyalty and pride. They are even secretly thrilled to know that they made the grade and so-and-so didn't.

The Fear and Intimidation leader does issue carrots as well as sticks. Getting a word of public commendation from this leader can be worth several hugs from the Good Old Boy leader. In their own slightly aloof way, the intimidating leader will, in time, show their pride and affection for the loyal and elite staff. Making fear and intimidation work for them, this strong and dominate figure gains the respect and admiration from his whole work force, who tends to foster a hunger for approval. This powerful leader develops a staff and sales team into a unique core of people who are constantly motivated and challenged. This in turn results in an organization that outperforms any and all competition.

....

"If you are afraid to act, then you'll be afraid to lead."

ROBERT NASH, KANSAS CITY, MO

....

The Rah-Rah Master Leader

The Rah-Rah leader, or we can call him the Razzle-Dazzle leader, will get his whole staff excited and enthusiastic about team goals, sales, productivity, customers, and life itself. He is not merely Mr. Optimism, he is more like Reverend Optimism. When everyone feels low at an early office meeting, he takes over and immediately gets things turned around. This great leader's enthusiasm is infectious. It is no wonder that everyone likes to be around him. If brought into a sales division or accounting office where things seem depressed, chaotic, or just plain unsuccessful, he will, more likely than anyone else, get everything moving in a right and positive direction.

The Rah-Rah leader's fire also has an effect on dull customers. When, for example, a salesperson needs help getting a sale from a "laidback" customer, all the salesperson has to do is call in the Rah-Rah leader to T.O. (take over or turn over) the sale, and then just watch this so-called difficult customer's reaction. The result is like a bolt of lightning. All of a sudden, a new and powerful surge of energy is at the closing table, and chances are more than likely the reserved and hesitant customer will get involved in the enthusiasm and purchase the product, amazing everyone in the office.

Like Reverend Optimism, the Rah-Rah leader keeps the energy level turned on high by having complete faith in himself and his maker. His line of product he sells is "good news," and he wants his staff and salespeople (his apostles) to be downright evangelical about it.

To this leader, a sales campaign becomes a crusade and his sales meetings his pulpit. At staff and office meetings, he'll jump up and down, clap his hands, or even sing out loud. This excited leader can make employees feel good about beating the competing dealerships or corporations. Not everybody can keep up with 8:00 a.m. to 6:00 p.m. smiles and firm handshakes, but the bottom line is that he produces great overall results. Most everyone associated with him not only makes money, but is happy and excited while doing it.

....

"Leaders want their employees excited about tomorrow because of their work today."

LINDA SALAS, BANNING, CA

....

The Negative Master Leader

Reader, don't let this title mislead you. This kind of leader is a far cry from being negative, but he does demonstrate negative approaches in his leadership role. He uses a lot of reverse psychology on his office staff and salespeople. For example, at a meeting he'll tell everyone that they have to reach a certain goal by the end of two days and then, before closing the meeting, he'll add that he wouldn't be surprised if everyone fell short of the intended goals, that they might not have it in them to meet the challenge. In other words, he gets everyone motivated to prove him wrong and illustrate what they can do themselves.

On a personal level, he will privately tell a staff member that he is very disappointed in his production or efficiency, then he'll add, like an afterthought, "I sincerely thought you were stronger and better than that, Mr. Employee. I guess I was wrong. I overestimated you." Unless the dressed down employee is a real mess-up, he likely responds with a superlative effort to earn the raised eyebrows and affirmative nod of his leader.

These two simple illustrations help you see where the term "negative" comes from to describe this bold and manipulative leader. One couldn't get more opposite of the Rah-Rah leader's mode of operation. The Negative leader uses intimidation of a different sort—getting employees motivated to avoid shame and prove their self-worth.

This master leader produces solid results without overt methods like threatening job security. Instead, he subtly plants thought seeds in the employee's mind. He makes the employee realize on his own that he really can do a much better job. The Negative leader senses which employee would have the most productive reactions to his devious implantations. He's a learned PhD of in-your-face psychology, treating his staff and salespeople like patients. Now, most of these "patients" do get better, and the company's sales figures get teased, prodded, and provoked to new and greater heights. This special leader is not a very excitable person and, compared to the Rah-Rah leader, he barely seems to breathe, but he never gets flustered when things go wrong. Quite the contrary, he is calm and quiet, always looking for a sound and fair solution to any internal office problems or outside interference.

He always stays level-headed when most emotional leaders run around, making matters worse. When things go right for the whole company, sales division, or an individual, the Negative leader says nothing, but just nods his head in approval and displays a slight smile. Somehow, that small positive gesture from the Negative leader seems to say it all, and any employee who witnesses it will be charged from that little acknowledgement for weeks to come.

"Salespeople expect more from their leaders
than they do from themselves."

CHARLES LANE, OGDEN, UT

The Playboy Master Leader

How this leader does his job, no one seems to really know, but he does it and he does it well. The Playboy leader basically has a lot of fun. He motivates through excitement and good times as effectively as the intimidating leaders do through fear or shame. He enjoys his work and his play, sometimes both at the same time. But again, what can you say? The so-called higher-ups can't complain because his office staff and sales force's performance are excellent. No matter how tired he ought to be after a long weekend or a late night escapade, he always has his business under control and in proper order.

He can't be accused of corrupting anybody in the office with his hedonistic ways because he is too clever, smart, and discreet to social-ize with company personnel beyond the bounds of company parties. Back at the office, the Playboy leader is always exuding the cologne of charisma. His office and sales teams eagerly perform at their best to better bask in their leader's popularity and dream that they could someday be like him. This particular master leader is indeed a rare breed. He combines a true happy-go-lucky personality with good solid business sense. He can sell his ideas and the company's products with the best of them, using little more than his infectious charm. He knows, and uses, all the secrets of professional salesmanship that get contracts signed, but he never lies or distorts the truth. He inspires his office staff and sales team to do likewise even though they may lack his natural abilities to sweet talk and enchant. True, some of his employees don't really know how to take this type of leader. Maybe there's some jealousy going on, or no one can figure out just what makes this Playboy leader tick. Whatever differences exist between a few employees and this unusual kind of leader doesn't really matter in the long run because the bottom line for everyone in the company is this leader produces and performs. Remember, the Playboy man-ages to succeed while having such a good time because his smile and positive attitude are real.

He is genuinely happy to see his co-workers in the morning. It doesn't matter that his joy feeds on the adoration of his staff because there is usually plenty of cheer to go around. He sincerely likes work as much as play, and he can make selling and productivity as much fun as a tennis match or world tour adventure. Those who might resent his dominant popularity get won over by his influential personality and knowledge of international business. If this particular leader doesn't handle the minute details as well as the By-the-Book leader (see below), it doesn't matter. There is always someone eager to help the Playboy leader out. Because things are usually in such good shape, he can afford to take that extra morning off to play golf or leave early to go wining and dining with clients. While some of his detractors feel that his mind isn't solely on business, the Playboy surprises people by reading up on professional sales and management insights. He is a true pro who fully and willingly accepts his responsibilities to his entire staff and of course to his company.

Just for one minute, let productivity fall off and surprise! This leader will suddenly appear from nowhere with enough fire and force to get things squared away fast! As much as he loves entertainment, the Playboy leader likes making money, not only for himself, but for all his employees. Who better than this type of leader to get the message across that great progress and superior sales will pay for a lot of good times?

> *"Don't talk about your mistakes, others will."*
> CHRIS FOWLER, RICHMOND, VA

The By-the-Book Master Leader

This particular leader couldn't be more different than the Playboy. She doesn't really seem to know how to have, or give, any spirit of excitement to others, except when it comes to payday.

The By-the-Book, or the Nuts and Bolts leader, doesn't often smile so the loyalty between her staff members and sales team tends to be on a purely financial basis rather than a personal or mentor cornerstone. This type of regimented leader is strictly a company person. While the firm's staff members working directly with her accomplish their career objectives to the maximum, this leader's strong company allegiance and devotion dampens any sincere or genuine relationship that could, or should, exist between a true leader and their employees. Now, the employees do have a great deal of respect for

this corporate-minded leader, and that in a nutshell is the key ingredi-
ent allowing the By-the-Book leader to excel.

This leader gets along best with the professionals around her who
can understand and appreciate her quiet and reserved competence.
This master leader lives up to all of her corporate responsibilities. She
is not lazy, untrustworthy, or a backstabber, just a leader who makes
and follows orders to the letter. It's guaranteed that no other leader
beats her at that. As smart as she is in the business sense, she falls
short when it comes to interpersonal relations or "people sense." Many
times this leader is resented for being too much of a "Yes" person, but
in all fairness, is always truthful and evenhanded with people. When
a sales or staff member approaches this leader in a time of real need,
this company-oriented master will usually pull through. Her heart
isn't entirely locked up in the company safe.

In general, all staff personnel maintain a level of respect for this
leader who, whether right or wrong in her assessment of a problem,
will always show instantaneous and firm convictions in her decisions.
Even if she's too consistent for some tastes, she will soundly take a
stand on an issue and never allow a problem to escalate via a series of
inconclusive staff meetings. Her predictability is dull to some but very
stabilizing and comforting to others. Sometimes viewed as an endan-
gered species in the business world, the By-the-Book leaders are
much appreciated by the more conservative employees who don't
mind sticking strictly to the rules given to them by the company.

Any employee who works for this type of leader and feels that a
firm's guidelines or rules are made to be bent or broken had better
check the help wanted ads before they find themselves in the predicament of looking for a job while out of one.

These leaders are not easy to work for or with and are nearly
impossible to befriend. But in truth, any employee who can put up
with this leader's all-work-and-no-play attitude can thrive professionally, reaching goals never before imagined.

....

"To get an employee to love his job, you make him successful at it."

L.C. COULTER, NASHVILLE, TN

....

The Teacher Master Leader

Any corporation, company, or sales force on this earth would be more than fortunate to have a leader like this aboard. The Teacher leader is viewed in the business world as one of the best. Not only is he professional at his job, but he takes his extra time to share his wisdom and leadership knowledge with others. He is a sound and understanding instructor who will always sit down with employees and explain in detail any company position, product, or sales tactic. This leader will listen, try to relate, and express his true feelings on every subject. He is a very unselfish type who doesn't prejudge. He is not nor ever will be jealous of others' success. Unlike some run-of-the-mill executives who like to rule over people, the Teacher leader is genuinely happy for the advancement of others in his firm. He is a cheerleader who wants all to be the best they can be.

This kind of leader keeps the everyday flow of new product and sales information circulating around the entire office so other leaders, or managers and their teams, can learn and grow, thus benefiting the whole corporation. He's the ideal educator to break in a new staff member, salesperson, or fellow executive because he is an eternal student of business practices. He honestly understands salespeople because he remains one himself. The Teacher energetically helps anyone with a professional or personal problem. He feels it is part of his job.

This leader can educate because of his years of experience. In fact, he would be one of the top salespeople in the company if he were to return to the sales force. He is not one of those administrators who has lost his selling skills and hides behind a desk and title. This kind of exceptional leader is hard to find, and there is not a salesperson anywhere who wouldn't gain valuable insights by listening to and taking notes from this gracious, talented person. Now, this doesn't mean everyone in the firm likes the Teacher leader. There will always be a few private types of people who actually resent this leader and their style. To the majority of the company's employees, however, the bonds with the Teacher are those of gratitude. Everyone in general is thankful that this leader is so often, and so skillfully, minding their business.

"People need to be told they are important, or they will forget it."
JIM HUNSINGER, AUSTIN, TX

The Positive Can-Do Master Leader

This leader differs in many ways from the Rah-Rah master leader mentioned earlier. True, the Positive Can-Do leader always has a good, healthy outlook on business and life, but he demonstrates the attitude in a quiet, calm manner. This kind of leader won't be found running around the office patting everyone on the back or working to get everyone's adrenaline flowing. That's not his or her style. In fact, he's more like the mirror opposite of the Negative leader. He'll look an employee in the eye and say, "I know you can do it. I depend on you."

Instead of motivating with reverse psychology, the Positive Can-Do leader motivates and inspires by having a slow, deliberate, and steady air about him, kind of like a tortoise that always beats the hare. This type of leader will, at his own pace, quietly walk around the firm with a pleasant smile, interested in the good of everyone. He takes his time to listen to anyone's problems or suggestions and will do all he can to help or move an idea along. He works wonders with unhappy customers and can give a depressed employee a ray of redemptive sunshine along with a few quiet words of encouragement and wisdom. If, for example, a salesperson is in a slump, this kind of leader will emphasize the best things about the salesperson or his stellar past performance, giving praise when he needs it most. The Positive Can-Do leader is an asset to his company because he turns any troubling situation into a challenge that can and will be overcome. Instead of playing employees against each other to increase productivity through competition, this type of leader tries to keep everyone working together harmoniously. He has an uncanny eye for spotting and defusing trouble between staff members. While he is too low-key for some, this leader wins over most of his employees by combining some of the affection of the Good Old Boy leader with some of the guidance of the Teacher leader. Most of the company's personnel will do anything to keep close to this Positive Can-Do leader because they want to soak in his self-confidence and optimism, not only for themselves, but for the office environment.

....

*"I didn't think I was a leader until I turned
around and saw people following me."*

Bill Owens, Memphis, TN

....

Reader, the master leaders just outlined will give you a pretty good idea of the many different and engaging personalities that make up this highly specialized professional. The leader, no matter what kind of interesting personality he has, is the very backbone of any organization or corporation. Without strong, charismatic, and/or pace-setting directors, the firm's employees, no matter how good they are, would not be as organized or productive as they could be. The master leader is blessed with a good measure of courage and determination, and he or she uses these qualities to lead men and women along the exciting path of success.

....

"You either live your dreams or someone else's."

Darcy Malone, Pittsburg, PA

....

2. The Special Makeup of a Master Leader (The Leadership Principle)

There are as many ways to become a master leader as there are people with different qualities who want to become professional leaders. The only common denominators are excellence and that special principle called the Self-Igniting Leadership Element. All the profiles of leaders include the ability to motivate and encourage oneself, then when the spirit is strong, to reach out and help others.

A master leaders special ability to self-motivate enables the them to always be a step ahead of the crowd when it comes to reaching goals and meeting responsibilities. This extremely important Self-Igniting Leadership Element can also be described as a powerful inner belief in oneself, a faith so strong that it inspires others to believe in themselves. To be an effective leader, one's character must *innately* contain a spark of this Self-Igniting Leadership Element. There are no textbook skills in the world that will compensate if one wants to become a true leader rather than a competent middle management person. Again, we sincerely hope that readers can find their path to leadership mastery within the pages of this book and learn to fan their inner sparks of ambition in to this self-igniting flame than can transform one into a torch bearer. (See Chapter 4, "Preparing Employees and Salespeople for details on how one can achieve and utilize this magical Self-Igniting Leadership Element.) On the way to achieving leadership excellence, it is important to note the personal and educational background of a master leader.

....

"If I can't discipline myself, then how can I discipline others?"

GARY TURNER, LOS ANGELES, CA

....

3. THE MASTER LEADER'S BACKGROUND

Reader, have you ever wondered why the great leaders of the world continually succeed throughout the challenges, setbacks, surroundings, or quagmire they find themselves in or inherit? Why and how do these master leaders of others, regardless of their background, have the ability to overcome obstacles, rise to the occasion, and promote new growth when the circumstances they acquired or persons they replaced didn't?

Well, the answer is pretty simple: true successful leaders believe in their goals and what they are doing more than they believe in anything else on earth. They have their spiritual faith to lean and depend on, and they have their deep-seated ideas and wants that are so real and obtainable that they are willing to give all. Leaders of men are unshakable in their beliefs and devotion. They will fight for what is right and never give up or give in. Master leaders win because they know what they are doing is the honorable thing for all concerned, and no one, or any situation, will destroy or claim victory over that sacred spirit.

Now, to become a great leader, it must be recognized that there are no MBA, PhD, or other formal educational requirements needed. Of course, the more education the better, but truthfully, the best "degrees" are earned and won in the real world's school of hard knocks. (Knocks on the door-to-door route or cold-calling will earn any person quite a few credits.) This degree that carries with it tremendous knowledge is called a "practical PhD." When broken down, it simply refers to being: Poor, Hungry, and Driven.

Every leader has his own unique story to tell in regard to his background and/or education. For instance, some leaders have never finished high school while others hold doctoral degrees from the finest colleges and universities in the world. (These degrees are not necessarily in business.) Some leaders come from stable and even wealthy families while others come from broken homes with no money. The calm of one's background might lead to becoming a Wall Street leader while the pain and emotional deprivation of a contrary personal history might propel another to become a Fear and Intimidation leader.

Qualitative variations in background don't really make that much difference in the long run. Manners, etiquette, poise, and sophistication can be learned by the most underprivileged person. All one needs is that spark of enthusiasm and the motivation to learn from others the skill to study successful people while developing one's own individuality and demeanor.

....

"Your habits, good or bad, will turn into your character."

UNKNOWN

....

Not counting what one's background or education has been, the person who does turn into a master leader has to have two extra ingredients that are not fully attainable through education. These key ingredients are: (1) total belief in oneself and (2) that wonderful, uncompromising quality called courage.

Note: There is no right age for a master leader. He or she could be a child prodigy of eighteen or a patriarch of seventy. It really doesn't make a difference, just as long as he knows his responsibilities to his entire staff and can carry them out professionally. A young person with exceptional poise can have the Self-Igniting Leadership Elements of self-confidence, self-motivation, and faith. The senior person may have developed those traits over a forty-year period in business.

Whatever the age or gender, kindness and wisdom will always be the needed safety nets utilized to prevail in battle.

Note: You can't run a prize-winning company by waving around your resume and bragging about your past successes. You might impress some office personnel, but salespeople and sales managers want to know what you've done for them lately and what you will do for them today? Salespeople, more than anyone, can tell immediately if a new leader is a winner or a loser. Now, all the fire-like imagery of a master leader's Self-Igniting Leadership Element is no accident. One can light a hundred torches from a single flame without losing any original fire. So it is with the special motivating fire of a leader: his flame of enthusiasm spreads throughout the office until everyone is reflecting a glow that in turn produces great results. The master leader knows for a fact that what you give out is exactly what you'll get back.

To leaders, belief in others is equally as important as belief in oneself. Even the Negative leader can project to his entire staff that deep down he knows they can do it, they can succeed. Belief in oneself without the skill and ability to kindle like feelings among the staff will only be interpreted as arrogance. No background history in the world will save a leader who comes off as self-centered rather than team-centered. If a master leader radiates arrogance, it is an expression that declares his team is the best and conveys excitement for his employees.

....

"I'll seek advice but always make the final decision and be responsible for the outcome."

JOHN ALLEN, PALM SPRINGS, CA

....

4. Common Sense and the Master Leader

Master leaders are not only intelligent when it comes to business and sales situations, but they also possess a great deal of good old-fashioned common sense as well. Without this sound "horse sense" going for the leader day in and day out, any sales organization or corporation anywhere would eventually self-destruct.

The leader has incidents that come up every day that cannot be solved by looking up the solution in some professional guidebook. Many such problems have to do with certain employees and sales-people and their unbelievable talent for getting into awkward or troubling predicaments. The leader has the everyday responsibility of getting the problems solved and squared away, and a leader succeeds in these matters by using his common sense. For example, if an employee is coming to work high on drugs or alcohol, the leader, with common sense in hand, will figure out the best move without resorting to an instant knee-jerk emotional reaction (such as immediate firing) or an overly deliberate approach based on some pop psychologist's "expert" advice. The true leader will measure up the situation for everyone's best concern. If, for instance, the troubled employee has never really produced for the company and is in a position to embarrass the firm, then common sense would dictate a discreet but very swift dismissal. If, on the other hand, the problem employee has given five years of good service to the company, then the leader must do what he can to retain the employee.

Here the leader has to rely on his personal knowledge of the individual. If the employee is the kind of person who can take it, the leader will ask them about their problem in the privacy of his office. The leader will show empathy on one hand, but firmness on the other. A probation period, if applicable, or an extended leave will be set for the employee to get cleaned up. Common sense tells the leader not to mention permanent dismissal as this talented employee could (all things are possible) turn around and utilize his or her talents and abilities for the competition. If the troubled employee could never survive an honest confrontation without quitting, the leader with common sense will have to improvise. The master leader will send a memo to the problem employee to the effect that their two-week paid vacation has been moved up to the next day. In addition, two weeks of unpaid vacation has been added on. No drugs or alcohol are mentioned, but the employee who reads, "We value your work and look forward to seeing you four weeks hence, looking and feeling like your old self again," will get the message loud and clear. Common sense now provides the employee with a "vacation" memo to save face and not feel too chastised to return to work after wrestling with and conquering his demons.

Common sense is not only a useful and powerful tool but a special gift that all masters value. The leader uses this "skill" gift for all kinds of situations in the same way a philosopher uses logic.

A master of common sense will:

A. Analyze the problem.
B. Seek council.
C. Weigh the alternatives.
D. Come up with a sound solution that best satisfies and benefits all parties involved.

Like the other qualities all leaders possess, common sense cannot be automatically learned in some classroom. It has to be acquired gradually in the experiences of everyday living. A leader comes fact-to-face with new and challenging problems every day, including personal trouble and business difficulties. The only way he is going to come out on top is by clearing out emotional reactions, checking with his instincts, and employing his innate common sense. If a leader has to constantly look up answers, ask fellow workers for advice, or have meetings with his assistants to examine everything, then he had better resign and get another job. Because the one he has now will drive him to an early grave.

If you're a person who doesn't have a lot of common sense via the real world or can't develop any "horse sense" to pull the wagon on your own, then give it up. You'll never make it as a leader. The common sense of a leader doesn't come with a new office or better pay. If someone is hired as a leader but can't figure out things through common sense on their own, then they need to swallow their pride and tell the company to hire another person. The courage to make an important decision on the spot is the hallmark of a master leader.

In discussing a leader's characteristics and behavioral patterns, it should be stated that with all of his powers of inspiration, common sense, and courage, he is a human being. He has the same headaches and heartaches, the identical emotional and physical aches and pains as everyone else. The great difference between the leader and other people, in and out of the office, is how he handles everyday problems, victories, or dilemmas.

"It's not always easy, but I will be as strong as my employees expect me to be."

ANDY HERRERA, HOUSTON, TX

5. SELF-CONFIDENCE AND THE MASTER LEADER

The self-confidence of a leader definitely stands out. The leader thinks and acts differently from other folks because he is a genuine decision-maker, self-motivator, and problem-solver. For example, if he has to fly to an important meeting and the airline he's booked on goes on strike, he refuses to be grounded. If all the other airlines are booked solid, he will not just stand around like everyone else. He will either rent a car or rent a private plane if it benefits the company in the long run.

The master leader doesn't lose because he doesn't have that word "lose" in his vocabulary or mind. His take-charge personality is his badge of courage. The leader has the calculating thought process of a determined entrepreneur, yet the intuitive genius of a master artist. The leader combines his self-confidence with a willingness to take risks.

He bets on those he trusts with a prudent sense of knowing when to readjust if and when things start to go sideways. (A good military general knows when to retreat and fight another day.) The paradoxical qualities of positive thinking and practicality combined with courageous but empathetic emotions make the master leader a very unique breed.

Note: Very often a master leader's physical appearance will reflect the characteristics of determination, self-assuredness, and kindness. He walks with a leader's confidence; he stands straight with a posture of conviction; and his eyes twinkle with a genuine consideration and curiosity for others. Line up a leader with a group of commuters, and he'll stick out just like a two-star general in an office full of businessmen. It can be pretty well guaranteed that the general and the master leader will be recognized in a crowd without their attire revealing their profession.

6. The Behavior of a Master Leader

The leader tends to be a little too strict and demanding when it comes to his wife and family. In other words, he's not the easiest person to live with. The leader has a habit of bringing his work, and too often his troubles, home with him. This practice doesn't help his relationship with his loved ones at all. Now, this is not a wholesale condemnation but rather an observed generalization. Of course, an exceptional leader can be an ideal husband, father, wife, or mother, but there is a propensity for displaying the leader's everyday management skills upon opening the front door of the home.

The master leader would like his family to run as smoothly as he runs his office or firm. Ranging from expectations of ideal behavior from a spouse and children, to a limited (due to a hard day's work) contribution on the leader's part at home, is it any wonder why resentment often builds up on both sides? It is hard for the family to understand that the master leader eats, sleeps, and breathes his profession and position. It is practically impossible to get him to file away and forget all of his sales and business emotions the minute he walks into his own home. He is an expert at masking emotions that would harm his relationship with clients, employees, or other executives, but when his tie comes off at home, he is liable to unintentionally unload stored negative emotions and frustrations on the souls he loves most. Of course taking one's business home is not a description of emotional and psychological baggage. Many leaders' personal time is disrupted by the ever-present problems of assistant managers, fellow executives, or employees. Even if all phones are turned off, the leader may take home important reports to read or re-write for the next day's staff meeting. Just when one of his children needs help in a school assignment or the in-laws are in the neighborhood and decide to drop by at home, this very calm and collected professional diplomat might be susceptible to irritability and subtle outbursts.

Well, in his defense, the leader is human, and there must be some safe place where he can go and no longer have to behave like a super-human crusader. Things at home will always go a lot smoother if the family and leader can understand and realize how much tension and anxiety have been bottled up in the office all day long. A master leader really needs his family to lend positive support and lots of love. The family must acknowledge that a true leader is a person who has been giving out a great deal of energy, consideration, and attention to others during his working day. And, in turn, the leader knows deep down in his heart that the only source great enough to replenish that spent power is his family and his maker.

....

"Temptation always wants to be my friend."

DAVID STEWART, HATTIESBURG, MS

....

7. THE MASTER LEADER'S SOCIAL LIFE

When the leader attends a social function or public gathering, whether or not it's for his corporation, he appears a different person altogether. In general, he seems more relaxed and low-keyed in this social setting than at the office or even in his own home.

There are several reasons for this changed behavior. First of all, when the leader is out socially, he can wear the badge of director, executive, or boss without being weighed down by its responsibilities. He can also, for the moment, relax and forget figures, reports, and performances even if the function is a sales party attended by the whole sales force. Instead of projecting an authority figure, he can sit back and listen to others and quietly bask in any and all glory like a well-fed lion. He will mingle congenially with the crowd and truly enjoy himself but never completely let down his guard or lose control. A leader won't let alcohol or any other temptation get the better of him or let some friendly enthusiasm loosen his tongue with foul language. Leaders are extremely aware of those jealous people in the organization who are constantly watching and waiting for them to make a mistake or create a spectacle of themselves. Unfortunately, there are always envious vultures circling overhead in the hope that they can swoop down on a leader who makes some misstep.

Furthermore, the master leader does not forget for a second that he is a major representative of his company and that he is in the spotlight for all to see and examine. The leader will always put his best foot forward when in public and be a perfect gentleman or lady. In most any kind of social get-together, the leader will expertly work the crowd like a seasoned politician running for office. It is also interesting to note how diplomatic and noncommittal the otherwise strong-minded and decisive leader can be. He gladly talks to all, listens to all, and acknowledges all, while knowing, even in a festive atmosphere, he's still the boss.

"In truth, I just don't have time for failure."

LEE RASMUSSEN, SEATTLE, WA

8. THE MASTER LEADER ON HIS OWN

This fascinating species called the leader is also worth studying in those special moments of downtime. A master leader has a very high level of energy and can rarely be found, if ever, relaxing in a backyard hammock. If he is, then chances are he's got a sales report or other serious reading in hand. Not having a one-track mindset, the leader is likely keeping up on current events as well as pursuing a favorite hobby seriously.

Most leaders, believe it or not, actually like to be alone. They need those quiet times of seclusion to think and keep everything in their active life in proper perspective. A leader tends to enjoy long walks, motorcycle rides, fishing, or any other activity that lets him clear his head. Any leader who needs to be around people all the time to prop up his or her importance and worth has some very big problems in the field of self-confidence.

The master leader is not lonely when by himself because he knows and understands his goals in life and has that devotion and unstoppable drive to obtain them. This great passion alone is enough to keep him going even when everyone else is turning away or demonstrating ridicule. The leaders seek solitude to regain sanity, and to rediscover and rekindle that inner strength and power needed to go on being a dynamo. It might surprise some employees to see their leader at a house of worship or in deep meditation, but he has a real need to get in touch with a source of wisdom, vigor, and love beyond himself.

"The platform for all miracles is faith."

SHERRY JEFFERY, NEWPORT NEWS, VA

9. FIFTEEN IMPORTANT LEADER POINTS TO REMEMBER

1. No genuine master leader is afraid to make a decision or act. He is ready and willing to face the consequences himself. He will not, under any circumstance, blame his mistakes or miscalculations on someone else.

2. A master leader will always show courtesy and respect to everyone he meets, no matter how bad he might feel emotionally or physically. There is never an employee or customer so infuriating that the leader will blow up and lose his composure in a confrontation.

3. The master leader will know everything possible about customer relations, sales, office staff, and managers. He can and will, if necessary, help sell customers, write up contracts, file, serve food, make coffee, and act as the janitor, greeter,

doorman, and driver. He'll run errands, cheerlead, solve problems, and, in private, yell. The leader is all to all, and that credo will never fail him.

4. The leader never forgets that he is much more than just a boss to his employees. He knows and understands that he is a combination of a friend, parent, sibling, teacher, advisor, confidant, administrator, warden, and minister. He is always available to listen, help, suggest, inspire, and comfort. If an employee takes the time to search for the leader, then the leader had better take the time to be found.

5. The understanding leader takes it as a compliment, rather than an insult, when one of his employees accepts a managerial position at another company. It is also supreme flattery to discover that said employee is copying the leadership mode of his old boss.

6. A true leader will not envy or feel resentful toward another leader in the same company who has great success in sales, product production, or manufacturing. Rather than displaying such childish insecurity, the true leader will congratulate and be spurred on to a more intense but friendly rivalry.

7. A master leader lives every day to the fullest, always looking at problems as challenges and their solutions as his rewards. He carries this positive enthusiasm with him into every situation he faces. Now, is this a difficult mental exercise and task? You bet it is. But as the great thinkers say, "Your habits turn into your character." And by staying positive every day, the leader actually becomes a positive person—a human other people need and love to be around.

8. If the leader has had a rough time personally outside of the office, he will not, under any circumstance, bring that edginess back to the company. No large or small outside crisis will significantly affect his performance and effectiveness. The firm's employees never see their leader looking notably irritated, puzzled, or depressed.

Note: Reader, masking negative emotions and continuously carrying on in a positive light is not easy, so when you study leaders, remember that they are both great business people and actors and performers.

9.   The master leader measures the success of their company by the bottom line of closing percentages, sales volume, production performance, and by the overall attitude of his employees. If everyone believes they are on a winning team or feel they are a part of a caring family, then any glitches, slumps, or poor production periods can be comfortably examined, adjusted, and overcome. Attitude is everything, and the leader tries in every way possible to have all of his individual employees, as crazy as some are, work in harmony. When this agreeable working chord is found, business miracles happen day after day.

10. The true leader will always respect and keep any secret told to him by an employee. He can be counted on to safeguard conversations that are confidential. The leader doesn't gossip, whisper, or create problems for others. He is fair and trustworthy all the time, not just when he's on duty. This might sound too Boy Scoutish, but the truth's the truth. No one will ever be a great leader if they can't be trusted to listen, understand, advise, and keep quiet. If a leader has a reputation for telling all to all, no one will come to him with their problems, and he'll never get the truth about everything going on in the company. He'll have no one watching his back, no true friends, and, in a short period of time, no job.

Note: Only with the most severe or extreme illegal problems should the leader, after some deep soul-searching, risk breaking the bond of trust between himself and an employee.

11. The leader, even if he thinks he knows it all, will always take the time to listen attentively to any suggestions or ideas his office personnel, maintenance, security, errand people, or sales staff have to offer. No one is unimportant. If a leader thinks his title, no matter what it is, gives him the right to act like a big shot or untouchable, then this person is a phony, a

loser, and a disappointment to everyone. These descriptions are not too severe or rude, they're honest. Any person who thinks that some high-handed sounding title brings instant respect is a fool. Remember reader, leaders create their titles, titles don't create leaders.

12. The leader is, as mentioned before, a coach in many ways. They will be the first to encourage an employee when he or she is down in the dumps, the first one in line to congratulate someone on a job well done, and the first to dress down and kick some rear end when an employee has gotten out of hand or just plain old messes up. No leader is all positive or all negative. Leaders are a mixture of thinkers, planners, dreamers, and doers. Their genius is real and devotion hardcore. It's no wonder the company's employees stay on their toes when around the master leader; they never really know for sure what coaching personality will show up.

13. A master leader will never humiliate or criticize an employee in public. In sales meetings, the entire sales force, including the leader, can be yelled at and complained about, but individuals should never be called out on the public carpet. Firings, warnings, and serious talks should be executed behind closed doors. In the overall scheme of things, the goodness one person shows another is all that really counts. Leaders make hard decisions, but they always try to make those decisions with compassion and respect.

14. Every master leader should dress according to the dignity of his position. The leader should reflect his confidence and belief in his office and whole staff by his attire. Even if the Good Old Boy likes to get into short sleeves by rolling them up, he should at least arrive to work in a suit or appropriate outfit. The leader not only has to have class, he has to demonstrate it whether he likes it or not.

15. Master leaders are crafty and clever, and they have that great ability to get employees talking and eventually telling secrets not intended to be disclosed. Leaders have to have an ear to

the ground and eyes in the back of their head. They have to know what is going on around them all of the time or they'll lose control, respect, and eventually their job. Any leader who is worth his salt will not let anything big or little get past him. He will, as much as humanly possible, know everything that is going on in his company and with his employees.

Any time a leader starts to let little things slide or ignore situations that could, in time, affect everyone in his firm negatively, then that leader is on his way to losing everything he's worked for. When you're in a position to teach, guide, and help people with their future, then you had better take that responsibility seriously by putting your hands to the plow and, with truth and courage as your companions, press forward toward new challenges and victories.

Reader, by understanding in general the information in this first chapter, describing master leaders and their profiles, you should realize that anyone with spirit and determination can become, through hard work and discipline, a captain for others. All people, no matter their goals in life, need someone who is willing to cheer them on and advise. The road to success in business is littered with hopefuls who have given up on their dreams because there was no one there to encourages, push, pull, prod, or listen. Leaders are exceptional folks who put others first, believe in helping, and when times turn difficult, stand straight, face the elements, and say with confidence, "Follow me."

....

"Never laugh at another man's scars.
You weren't there for the wounds."

UNKNOWN

....

2.

Setting Up the Office

CHAPTER 2

SETTING UP

All leaders know if you are starting an office from the ground up, make sure your sales office is on the street level. Locate the sales department in an easy, flow-through, high-traffic location with good access to the rest of the firm's facilities. The office has to be convenient so customers are not overly challenged to follow directions, ask others, or get confused finding the exact place for their inquiries or appointments.

If you have inherited an office or company, then by all means, put your own signature on it with changes for the better. Make sure the office has good visual appeal and an inviting atmosphere. Look into indoor plants and colorful foliage arrangements to reduce the harshness and coldness of steel and contemporary lines. If you don't feel totally competent at interior decoration, then invest in a professional.

Don't forget, the outside of an office is the first thing customers and employees see. Your business should convey warmth, a family environment, and professionalism all in one quick visual statement.

Needless to say, but everything from the grounds, the corners, the floors, the walls, the work area, and everything else has to be spotless. Don't ever give others the chance to prejudge negatively before they have even said "Hello."

"Customers assume you are a professional. Don't ever create doubt."

MONTE SHELDON, NEW YORK, NY

---

1. THE OFFICE
(DRESSED FOR SUCCESS)

The interior of a leader's office, especially the furniture and wall colors, should reflect the same kind of solid confidence exuded by a trusting and solvent bank. No imitation wood grain desks, folding chairs, or pop interpretive artwork. The office should look and feel as though it will be there fifty years from now. It should offer customers and employees the feeling of a secure and respectable institution. Don't forget that the furnishings of a firm's office lend the same impression as a businessman's suit.

Leaders understand that a customer who feels comfortable, dignified, and somewhat pampered is easier for the salespeople to sell. Likewise, the employee who feels comfortable and proud will always produce more than a person who feels out of place, uneasy, and embarrassed. If your line of products has a showroom, don't make the mistake of having a beautiful showcase area and then a makeshift office. Don't ever assume that a customer is totally sold by the time he's approaching some desk to sign contracts. Even if the customer is favorably inclined to purchase, the size of his order or monetary commitment may easily plummet by a tacky sales cubicle or environment. Remember, every single detail that helps calm and relax a customer will only help increase sales. Any office or firm that utilizes this basic office information will in the long run be far ahead of the competition.

"Oversized" Design

In some offices, the company will purposely place oversized furniture in the reception area. This intentionally makes most customers or visitors feel physically smaller compared to the bigness of the furniture. This feeling of smallness works on the customer's subconscious mind by making his actions and thoughts less aggressive, bold, and egotistical. The bigness of the furniture overpowers the customer and puts him in a more humble and respectful mood. This oversized furniture tactic does work, but it must complement the office's architecture to look natural.

Office Colors

Colors are very important for any office, for the exterior as well as the interior. Never use a bright red or yellow as they only make most people cautious and slower in movement. Colors that will affect peoples' moods positively include colors like royal or navy blue, forest or light green, gold, and rich browns. There are also light, upbeat combinations that work such as cool pastels and desert-theme colors. Note that lavender and purples help people calm down if they are aggressive or irritable. Colors definitely affect employees' and customers' moods, and a master leader should get professional advice in choosing the right colors for his office.

"The mind interprets what the eye sees."

DR. T. MILLS COMPTON, NEW ORLEANS, LA

Refreshment Area

Have a special and appealing location in the office for refreshments. If nothing else, at least make sure that there is always water or fresh coffee available for visitors, customers, and employees. This little courtesy is very important. It allows you to show hospitality and consideration. Remember, every positive step that helps make people feel at home is a step toward progress. Public relations, employee efficiency, and sales or manufacturing are the company's bottom line, and the leader has to enlist every possible resource and strategy to be successful year after year.

Royal Restrooms

Always have extremely clean restrooms, especially for the ladies. Nothing can be more repulsive to a visitor, employee, or customer than to enter a dirty or unkempt restroom in an office.

The master leader should go to extra lengths to make sure that the restrooms are spotless and as well decorated as any other part of the office. The ladies' lounge, in particular, should be thoughtfully and tastefully appointed. Flowers and proper lighting always seem to add that needed touch too. Any little thing that might make someone feel uncomfortable will (it can be guaranteed) have a negative effect not only on attitudes, but business as well. Lastly, all employees must *walk* their customers to the bathrooms and never give out directions to it. A good dose of manners from the yester world will speak volumes…just try and see!

2. THE PRESENTATION ROOM

A leader's firm might have a sales office set up to facilitate simultaneous customer presentations. The leader may or may not have the luxury of separate sales offices, meeting rooms, or separate conference rooms, so there are several points to keep in mind.

The Closing Room (The Pit)

In a closing room or sales pit, keep the individual closing tables far enough apart so that each customer cannot hear the distinct conversations taking place elsewhere. The magic buzzing noise from a large room with a lot of talking creates excitement and a very positive sales atmosphere. Again, because it's important, never let customers get close enough to hear other sales presentations and negotiations at nearby tables. The customer will begin comparing one sales person's advice, price quotes, and financial arrangements to another. This not only disrupts a salesperson's presentation, but can and most likely will lead to customer resentment and bad feelings as well.

Beat the Clock

Do not put clocks on the walls of your presentation and/or closing room. Just as casinos don't want to advertise what time of day it is, don't make it too easy for a customer to think about the time and being somewhere else. The leader has to keep his customers intrigued with his products and salespeople's presentation. The time it takes to close a sale is something leaders don't want on a customer's mind.

> *"Any person put in a formal environment will act, or try to act, formal."*
>
> BRUCE BIDWELL, PHOENIX, AZ

Sitting at Attention

Unlike the overall office, the leader doesn't want his sales closing room to be living-room comfortable. Plush chairs and soothing music will make customers overly relaxed at a time when they should be alert and attentive to their buying decisions. The chairs in the sales pit should be wooden and straight backed. Some sales offices use chairs with arms on them so the customer can rest and avoid having to fold his or her arms, which, of course, generates a negative and defensive attitude.

No Distractions

Keep all worksheets, papers, sales materials, contracts, financial forms, applications, etc. close at hand but *not* in plain view of the customer. Any sales materials that are unnecessarily lying around will only have an adverse effect on a customer. Once the customer is sitting at the closing desk, he often has his defenses up and is just waiting for an excuse to express an objection. For example, "Mr. Salesman, you suggested the financial terms in Plan A, but according to your company's brochure I just found on your desk, there seem to be better terms for me in Plan B." The carefully built-up momentum of the salesperson has been disrupted by sales materials he unintentionally left on his desk, information he did not, for whatever reason, want his customer to see. Reader, also remember that a blank contract or worksheet lying around could similarly intimidate a customer in the way a hypodermic needle sitting on a doctor's desk can unnerve a patient. To ensure that a salesperson produces what he wants when he wants it, have an uncluttered closing table where all sales materials are close but out of sight and reach of the customer.

The Closing Table

There are several schools of thought concerning closing tables. Many leaders and professional salespeople prefer the intimacy of a round table, while others prefer the authoritative presence established by rectangular or square ones. With a round table, a salesperson can lean toward a more eager spouse or business partner and establish a two-against-one majority to press for the sale. When the salesperson is likely to confront two or more resistant customers, a square table with chairs spaced appropriately apart is preferable. This way the salesperson won't feel surrounded by the difficult customer with his objections and/or outbursts. Again, the square closing table will put the salesperson in a better position to hold firm and negotiate with less intimidation or intimacy. No matter the closing table's shape, the table had better be stable and robust. The deal will feel like a backroom swindle if it's consummated on a rickety card table. Make the closing table as trustworthy as a good banker's desk.

....

"Your surroundings are silent, yet ever-telling ambassadors."

SUSAN BROCK, LAS VEGAS, NV

....

3. Running a Professional Office/Sales Office

Don't Use Time Clocks

There is no reason to use time clocks. If a master leader can't get his office staff to arrive on time for work or discipline them for breaks or errands during the work day, then he's not worth having as an executive. Time clocks might have their place in a large factory, but not in a professional office or sales office. Every person who works in the office should possess the same enthusiastic winning spirit of their leader and want to be on time and accountable.

It is true that when the cat's away the mice will play, but the leader is a tiger, not a little house cat. A time clock only lends a rat race mood to what should feel more like a sports clubhouse or a military war room. Any employee who works with the leader and has to punch a time clock will, in the long run, end up just killing time.

4. How to Treat Office Personnel

The master leader will always treat everyone who works for him with the greatest respect. The leader, in order to achieve maximum results from his people, will use what is called the CEO Advantage. That is:

C = Consciously
E = Empowering
O = Others

This formula is utilized every day by great leaders. Leaders empower their employees through their own actions. In other words, leaders lead by example. They consciously make everyone who works for them feel extraordinary. When a culture of mutual respect, care, and concern are created, and true relationships are built for the betterment of everyone, every single employee beings to function at a much higher level. Just think for a minute, what would any organization look like if each and every employee began to operate 10 percent more effectively across the board? How would the employees feel?

Success, growth, and respect are all contagious, but so are laziness, negativism, and discontent. Leaders invest their time in their employees so everyone feels important, needed, and appreciated.

Leaders also understand that their employees know their responsibilities and that certain levels of expectation are held over them. Yet few employees feel that what they do truly makes a difference in the overall scheme of things. Additionally, if an employee's agenda is to simply show up for work, navigate from any trouble, and be as minimally important as possible without intervention, then they will. Conversely, if an employee is met by a super leader and encouraged to deliver their best and depended on to make a positive difference, then—boom!—that employee will heed the call and produce while feeling great about him or herself. He'll be proud he made the leader proud. Investing in the personal agendas of employees is just sound and smart. The leader understands that ultimate success lies in the hearts and minds of his people and the quicker he begins to champion his employees, the faster the door of victory opens.

"People know my name, but only God knows my soul."

JERRY SPICER, CHICAGO, IL

5. NAMES COUNT, NOT THE POSITION

From the very day we are born, the one thing each and every person has that separates them from all others is their name. The name we are given is our personal identity granted to us by our parents. Simply put, a lot of so-called leaders overlook this important and personal asset. Master leaders know the names of their employees, and they know their positions. True leaders care, and the first step in showing that is knowing everyone's name.

6. THE OFFICE MANAGER DEFINED

The office manager is not the sales manager or the master leader. He or she is in the firm to keep all paperwork and regular day-to-day office procedures running smoothly. In a busy company, the sales managers would be lost without a competent and trustworthy office manager. The office manager should keep track of all records and sales contracts so that the leader is free to proceed with his job of having everything and everyone working in tandem and, of course, keeping the sales department positive and productive. The office manager works for the master leader, not the other way around. When an office manager thinks that he or she can run a professional office and sales team better than the leader, then the whole firm will suffer from this twisted chain of command viewpoint.

7. THE MASTER LEADER AND THEIR EMPLOYER

The leader, no matter how dominant a personality he might have, must acknowledge, if applicable, the respectable position of his boss. The boss (the owner, president, or CEO of the company), on his part, must recognize that the master leader is the expert in knowing and motivating his employees and salespeople. A true leader won't step on the brass' toes, and they, in turn, will respect his turf. There will be times, however, when the field marshal and chief of staff don't see eye to eye. When this happens, both parties should withdraw to their lines and observe if one of them happens to be overstepping their bounds just a bit. If a leader is producing good results, the owner should not keep him on a short leash. If the leader constantly wants to overturn corporate policies, then it is time for him to start his own company.

8. STAFF DRESS CODE

Unless there are only one or two individuals that need speaking to, the leader may have to impose a dress code for all people working in his office. The object is to have everyone in the firm looking clean and neat, reflecting success. There can be no excuses for sloppiness or uncleanness. Even if the leader has to inspect his troops every morning, the extra time and effort will pay off. Let the salespeople snicker, but when they look smart, they feel smart and sell smart. Everything and anything that helps the company's reputation not only increases sales, but makes all employees proud of their position and proud to be at work.

9. THE SIDEKICK LEADER
(THE MASTER LEADER'S PROFESSIONAL PARTNER)

Few master leaders can function successfully without a competent partner, sidekick, or right-hand man. The company's employees have many nicknames for this executive second in command, and most of them—flunky, go-fer, yes-man—are not as friendly as sidekick. Whatever the employees call him really doesn't matter. The sidekick leader has a very important function within the overall organization. Without this trusted ally, the master leader would be at a severe loss.

More than an understudy by bucking for promotion, the best sidekick encourages and supports the leader. The assistant manager, if you will, must carry out directives dependably and step in capably to take the helm when necessary. No matter how strong a personality he has, the sidekick must submerge any dominance to harmonize with his boss, the leader—just as the president of a company has to have his vice president and a talk-show host has to have his co-host. Every good marriage, too, needs one partner who can graciously compromise and let the other lead in his or her area of strength. In far too many cases, the sidekicks are mediocre managers who do not learn enough about leadership from the master they work with. Ideally, the sidekick should consider himself the head of the sales department but with one man or woman above him.

In the chain of command, the sidekick is the first lieutenant and the leader is the captain. In the best of armies, companies, and sales forces, the troops don't miss a beat when the commander (the master leader) is out of action. Especially if the leader's absence is temporary, the competent sidekick should try to maintain the same pace and tone of work so that productivity doesn't lag in the confusion of a different tempo. The *only* time a sidekick should gradually change the mode of operation to suit his own style is if he is being promoted to the top spot.

"All master leaders need someone they can depend on."

TEDDI O'SHEA, GREENSBORO, NC

The company and sales force differ from the army in that there is no officers club to isolate the assistant leader (the first lieutenant) from the employees and salespeople (enlisted men). The sidekick is free to circulate among employees and salespeople and check up on any and all problems, situations, or rumblings. It is his (the assistant leader) job to solve or mediate any trouble before that trouble gets too big and disrupts the work flow. The best sidekick can smooth things out without appearing to favor the master leader or employees. When the sidekick does take sides, he will most always be in the master leader's corner. (In truth, he has to be if he wants to keep his job.)

The sidekick leader can always enjoy freedom of movement throughout his company as long as he doesn't get himself pegged as the boss's lackey. He must show empathy for all employees with a grievance, and openly defend them in the face of the owner even if he feels that they may be wrong.

The sidekick must make it clear that he is not the master leader and that he does not have the final word. This will prevent an employee from getting upset with the assistant leader when discussing the problem at hand. All employees should feel that the sidekick is their reliable ally to pass their complaints, suggestions, or arguments along to the master leader. Now, it takes some doing for the assistant leader to convince both the employees and salespeople that he is a true advocate for their side in a dispute, but these are the kinds of skills that will keep him at number two until the top spot is open.

The professional sidekick should know the overall operation of his company, its routine, and all responsibilities so he can lead when called upon. For instance, the assistant leader could be the person who takes roll call at sales meetings. He is the audience warm-up man for the leader's morning meetings, and he ought to know enough about important company topics to give some intelligent background material. He makes sure that all the sales contracts are signed properly and all paperwork is in order. If the support staff and secretarial pool do not have their own designated team captain, then the sidekick has to play that roll as well.

The assistant leader has to listen to all of the middle managers' and employees' gripes, war stories, and bad jokes. He has to put up with his boss's (the master leader) emotional needs as well as his business needs. It could be harrowing to play second fiddle to the Fear and Intimidation leader, and it might be fun to be a satellite of the Playboy leader.

Of course employees and salespeople come in a wide assortment and some have the talent for getting into strange predicaments all the time, but the assistant leader can't just call in the MPs. He'll have to settle the problems himself and get things back in good working order, along with a positive team spirit.

The sidekick will always have one very important job requirement that is never discussed openly and will never appear on a job description. He has to protect and watch out for the master leader's blind side, guarding the leader's back from any derogatory statements or negative opinions that might circulate from within the sales force or company. Any harsh and jealous allegations or vicious rumors may have sprung from petty rivalries, or serious incidents. But no matter where they came from, false and hurtful talk could, without the sidekick's intervention, undermine the effectiveness of the master leader and/or disturb sales and product production.

Note: The sidekick should never think that a wave of discontent or scandal will carry him to the top.

As well as being the master leader's chief of intelligence, the number two man has to be alert for any developments that could come between the hierarchy and his boss. The timely execution of some tiptoe diplomacy might well save a leader's job when careers are on the line. As one can see, the assistant leader has many important functions that help keep the company running productively.

He or she is much more than a nursemaid, peacekeeper, and friend to the employees and master leader. He is the person who keeps the office staff and sales force together so that the salespeople can do the job they know best (selling), the office staff can do what they know best (keeping progress moving), and the master leader can do what he does best (keeping everything and everybody positive, productive, and together).

"The future belongs to those who learn."

BRIAN KELLY, ORLANDO, FL

SETTING UP   43

Now, sidekick leaders come in as many varieties as the master leader himself. Let us explore three major types of sidekicks who have attained the level of master leader in their own right:

A. The Positive Sidekick.
B. The Negative Sidekick.
C. The Yes-Man Sidekick.

The Positive Sidekick Leader

This sidekick lights up the entire office with enthusiasm. He loves his work and does not feel apprehensive about his position or his prospects of rising up the managerial ladder. His contentment puts everyone around him at ease. It is needless to say, but the positive sidekick is very confident and skilled in his public relations abilities.

This type of assistant leader may be more talented than his boss, but he never lets on that he is thinking about or deserves the top spot. When his initiative is needed, he'll gently prod the master leader along with charm and good timing so that the boss is unaware that his assistant is quietly calling the shots. Just as the sidekick knows how much he and the boss can push individual employees, the Positive assistant knows how far the master leader can be pushed.

The Positive sidekick leader has no enemies. The employees and sales team feel that he is a friend and defender in any difficulties they might have with the master leader. This assistant leader works over-time to maintain unity between employees and management and between the salespeople themselves. The Positive sidekick wants only to keep everyone in the company geared up for success with no energy spent on negative squabbling. This kind of assistant leader tries to keep both his boss (the master leader) and other employees in an environment that feels professional and safe with his everything-will-be-okay personality; his style makes him a very valuable asset to the firm.

....

"The leader who seeks glory is illuminated in anguish and anxiety."

PAUL WENZ, MADISON, WI

....

The Negative Sidekick Leader

On the surface, it looks like this type of sidekick leader dislikes his job, fellow employees, and even customers. This Negative assistant leader usually has an emphatic "No!" for anyone who wants to try a new idea, sales approach, or who needs help with personal finances. All this negativism is his way of setting up an intimidating front that gives him a fairly smooth and even run with his subordinates. When any employee finally does get an affirmative response or positive comment, he or she becomes supercharged by the unexpected approval. Keeping his employees psychologically hungry for his blessings keeps them financially well fed, working and earning their maximum.

The Negative sidekick is a natural at what he does. It would be disastrous for another to attempt to imitate his method and style. This kind of masterly assistant not only wins, over a period of time, the begrudging loyalty of his employees, but is appreciated and respected by his superiors as well. This type of assistant leader could never be a Positive or Rah-Rah sidekick; instead he needs to work with either a subdued management group or one that does not clash with his uniqueness.

The Yes–Man Sidekick

Just as the name implies, he's the master leader's biggest ego booster. The Yes-Man sidekick is more than a competent executor of the master leader's orders; he is a skilled doer as well.

He knows the company's product well enough to T.O. (take over) for salespeople. He also knows sales contracts and any and all paperwork inside and out and doesn't have to bother his superiors with procedural matters. He or she works long, dedicated hours and is on call twenty-four hours a day. Nonetheless, he always has the stored up energy and loyalty to back up his master leader when necessary. In fact, this type of assistant leader is a true master leader of his own accord. In spite of this sidekick leader's talent, the Yes-Man position is exactly what he wants at this particular stage in his life. He gets satisfaction out of being a superb assistant leader. When a higher position calls, he might be tempted to relocate or be promoted to another company. In the meantime, he cheerfully keeps in tune.

If the Yes-Man has any flaws, it may be in the area of public relations with his firm's employees. True, he helps his employees and will go out of his way to assist customers, but one can't get around the irritating fact that he is always in complete agreement with everything the master leader (his boss) has to say. No matter what the master leader is discussing, whether it's sales, politics, sports, or stale jokes, the Yes-Man assistant will most always second his boss's opinions and viewpoints.

It might also get on some employees' nerves that the Yes-Man prefers the boss's company on everything from fishing trips and motorcycle rides to formal dinner parties. Behind the Yes-Man's back, some employees sneer that the assistant leader drives the same kind of vehicle and wears close to the same suits as the master leader to curry favor. This servile tendency to mirror the boss cuts slowly and negatively into the office staff's respect for him.

Ironically, the major motivation for this sidekick's imitation of his boss is that deep down he wants to be liked and respected by the company's employees in the same way that they like and respect the master leader. As the Yes-Man grows into a top managerial position of his own, he will likely see that he can gain full respect for being just who he is and not for whom he'd like to be. Even before he evolves into a master leader in his own right, this type of assistant leader wins more admiration than he knows for always doing a great job for his employees.

Remember that the most unique, charismatic, and successful master leaders at some point spent similar periods apprenticing as an assistant. Just look at the world of professional sports. Most of the dominant head coaches in the N.F.L. today were at some time assistant coaches, following someone else's orders just a few seasons ago. Being a Yes-Man is not an incurable disease. However, it can be a career-long decision for someone who only feels most confident in the shadow of a dominant master leader.

....

"The shadow of responsibility follows me everywhere."

DAVID CHAPMAN, ATLANTA, GA

....

10. The Master Leader's Off-Hours

What are the duties and responsibilities of a master leader after he leaves his office? First, the leader is always on call because of his personal and administrative obligations to his employees. The professional leader is the one person everyone turns to whenever they need advice, consoling, encouragement, or some kind of financial assistance. Secondly, the master's hours away from his staff are still not his alone. He is constantly, with every turn or encounter, representing his corporation, firm, or company while forever looking and searching for new and better ideas that will help boost sales and overall company productivity. The leader is absolutely married to his profession, and many times his personal family might not appreciate this ongoing close relationship. The leader's children may want dad to loosen up a bit at a family outing, but the leader is a walking public relations asset for his firm even at the ballpark or on vacation. The master leader is a salesman at heart and a commander seven days a week. He, through habit, can never turn his powers of persuasion and charm off. You can (as everyone knows, and the old saying goes) "take the master leader out of his office, but you can't take the office out of the master."

11. Dealing with Office Gossip

The master leader must daily deal with petty office gossip and whispers that could quickly grow into a destructive wedge driven between employees. The first things that a leader must do, concerning gossip, is find out the source of the rumor, privately confront the person or persons involved, and separate fact from fiction. Then, the master should immediately address the problem and get it stopped in its tracks (quelling any falsehoods) before they get out of hand and plague the positive flow of office performance. The intelligent leader knows when to discreetly call for outside help, like counselors or lawyers, and when to try to smooth things over himself. Even if some rumor proves untrue, the leader must know when it is the right time to arrange for the transfer or firing of a particular employee who keeps causing too many troubling distractions. The master leader has to have his finger on the pulse of his company's employees all the time, but this could be difficult for the more aloof types of leaders who are not very close to their staff. In this case, the master leader will often develop an agent for intelligence gathering. This agent is often the assistant leader or some trusted veteran employee who serves as the eyes and ears of the master. This spy (there are no other descriptions) picks up on things and tells the leader so he in turn can pounce on the problem before it gets out of hand.

Timing can be especially important when a leader is faced with the quandary of having two of his personnel battling an in-house quarrel. The master leader will escort the feuding individuals quietly and calmly into his private office and sit them down in chairs facing each other (no table). The master leader will sit between them and to the side, like a referee, and let the combatants peacefully air out and settle their differences. This settling of the matter might take ten minutes or two hours, but it will all be worthwhile if the problem is resolved and both parties can shake hands. If things don't work out, the leader may have to decide on who was guilty or the trouble maker and give one or both parties their walking papers. The leader has to step in as a mediator early enough to prevent the entire office staff from taking sides and ruining the cooperative spirit so very critical to success.

"Hidden in the mechanics of success is sacrifice, consequence, and fulfillment."

JACK THORNTON, BOWLING GREEN, KY

12. KEEPING THE OFFICE IN SHAPE

All of the previous topics and discussions about decorating the inside of an office and maintaining a good visual effect for the outside would be vain if everything else was not kept up to date and managed. In keeping all areas of the office or firm in tip-top shape, the master leader has to have the final say and keep control. Sure, there are custodians on the premises, but the final keep-everything-professional responsibility lies with the leader. The leader has to have a handle on everything that goes on around his office whether flickering light fixtures are not being replaced or floors are dangerously slippery on Monday mornings.

Along with the bonuses for the salespeople, there should also be an environmental prize for the employee showing the most concern for the company's workspaces and grounds. The master leader encourages everyone in the firm to help police areas and note any problems that need to be corrected. Leaders never forget that selling a product, manufacturing a product, or rendering a service is an emotional and psychological exercise, and a clean, well-kept environment picks up everyone's spirits and fosters pride in one's office home. Remember, the customer is a guest in that home. Any doubts or uneasiness concerning hospitality, cleanliness, or professionalism will make a customer or visitor uncomfortable, which, in turn, only leads to frustration, disappointment, and failure.

13. How Master Leaders Start Their Year

The master leader will start his year with an extra dose of enthusiasm. The leader has to get everyone in his office excited about the New Year and keep them motivated right down to the very last minute of his selling and production calendar. Everyone works best in rhythm, and a master leader keeps his whole staff moving in step to the necessary pace of his campaign. The master leader knows in order to create positive momentum and put his organization on the right track, it's imperative for him to induce a spirited drive with creative and constant energy. A leader's very presence, urgency, impact of personality, and level of excitement, can be all that's needed to drive through seemingly impossible obstacles and achieve unprecedented results.

Truly successful master leaders use a phenomenon called S.T.E.A.M. to motivate and propel their employees. The concept of S.T.E.A.M. breaks down like this:

S = Superior
T = Thinking

E = Energizes
A = Accelerates
M = Maximizes

Now, the concept of S.T.E.A.M. comes from this fact: Water is extremely hot at 211 degrees but does little or nothing to create energy. Yet, if the temperature is raised one degree, the incredible power of S.T.E.A.M. is created and unleashes energy with exponential power. The exact same concept exists within any company, firm, or organization and must be tapped into to achieve the ultimate measure of success. Have you, reader, ever seen a company that is truly struggling in all aspects, e.g., sales results, profits, margins, client acquisition, recruiting, and training, and then out of nowhere a leader is introduced ninety days later and everything has turned around to the positive? Everything and everybody in the company is experiencing success. Isn't it amazing how this new master leader, making very few personnel changes, resurrected a dying company? Well, the leader used the S.T.E.A.M. concept. The leader knows as the teams of employees warm up, they, with his guidance, find that one extra degree, that one little degree required to exceed, and momentum is magically born.

How does any company needing help get turned around? The answer is a strong master leader and his or her ability to deliver S.T.E.A.M. The leader's impact, presence, flair, delivery, and tone will always have a great bearing on all employees. And if the leader gets everyone to understand the S.T.E.A.M. philosophy, then wonders happen. Sales go straight up, and everyone in the company is proud, prosperous, and happy.

Another surefire way for inspiring all employees is keeping good and reliable office staff around year after year. Nothing makes an office more solid and successful than steady, loyal, and dedicated personnel. Achieve this by showing them respect and letting them immediately know any important company policy decisions. This way the staff will feel involved. To keep productive employees coming back, the leader has to keep everyone enthusiastic about sales production, team operations, and even more importantly, about themselves. The master leader lets his people know that they are growing, not stagnating.

Their salaries and bonuses should reflect that, but another cost efficient way is via the staff's responsibilities. As the leader continually depends on his personal relationships with his loyal team, so should the sense that veteran employees have more say and more weight in decision making. The excitement at the start of a business year has to be charged with promise, potential, challenge, and confidence. At the year's end, there ought to be a high note of satisfaction and accomplishment felt by each and every person involved in the results that were achieved.

Note: In some companies, too many leaders unfortunately overlook employees that could, if given the chance, be the very bedrock of success. Some so-called leaders walk right by individuals who truly have the ability and desire for great works. It's sad that some leaders miss out on new ideas and revelations solely because they feel they are above these individuals. Now, in the mind of some of these leaders it might be education, experience, wealth, knowledge, lineage, or just pure arrogance that keeps them blind, but no one fact remains true. Today's ladder of success must allow anyone to climb it, regardless of their position. It's important that a leader understands a very key fact: all the employees who fill what are typically deemed trivial roles have one monstrous commonality: dependence on the leader. The leader must understand that this one common factor is a perfect and exciting door to walk through and renew growth, generate spirit, and more importantly, draft a new base for success for the whole organization.

"A leader is nothing if he is not everything to his people."

SHEILA APPLEGATE, TULSA, OK

3.

Hiring Employees

CHAPTER 3

THE MASTER LEADER'S EMPLOYEES AND SALESPEOPLE

When building up one's office staff and team of salespeople, there is nothing more important than gathering the finest professionals available. Any ordinary or everyday manager can look through resumes and hire on past records and other superficial criteria.

However, it is the master leader who uses instinct and savvy to get the people who will work best for his distinct style. Here are ten general points to follow when hiring staff and professional salespeople:

....

"Knowledge is important, but I also want happy people."

WILLIAM NAIRN, DALLAS, TX

....

1. TEN IMPORTANT HIRING POINTS

1. <u>Listen to the applicant's story</u>: When the master leader sits down in his office to interview a potential employee, the very first thing he has to learn is to be a good listener. There are basically two main reasons for this.

    First of all, the person being examined is nervous, and in his or her nervousness, he is liable to make uncharacteristic mistakes in telling the leader why he wants the job and why he's qualified for it. The leader should not present a list of predictable questions so the practiced applicant can perform on cue. The leader should just sit there (after some small talk), keep silent, and listen. The applicant will be forced to start talking and elaborate. This tends to pull him from his prepared sales pitch. The applicant will see that he's not bowling over the leader with his planned and recycled presentation. With only the prompt of "go on" from the leader, the hopeful employee is forced to either begin telling the truth or start making up things. Either way, in these circumstances some hidden facts about the person's background and personality will eventually come out.

    The second reason for the leader's passive listening stance is to see if the prospective employee knows his business and/or is an effective salesperson. By attentively listening and observing, the leader can learn a lot about the person sitting in front of him. Of course, the applicant would like to engage the leader in pleasant conversation and sell him on congeniality rather than business knowledge. The leader who doesn't fall for this trap can sit back and rate the facing person for his professional abilities as well as for his charm. Keep in mind when hiring salespeople that, when asked, 95 percent will admit that they left their last job because they didn't get along with management.

Note: One of the best ways to instantly get a feel about another's personality is to (out of nowhere) ask the applicant what his favorite TV show or movie is. The question will make the person step back for a second, but the answer will tell the leader a great deal.

2. Read the applicant's body language: When the leader is inter-viewing an applicant, he should notice everything about him, from his brand of watch right down to the shine or no shine on his shoes. The observant leader will notice if the person is well groomed or if he is suffering from a hangover or a hard life. Any master leader should be able to detect anything in or out of place within minutes of their first meeting. When listen-ing to the pace and pitch of the applicant's voice, the leader does not for one second forget to also read the language of the prospect's eyes, hands, and body movements.

    If the applicant's eyes keep darting around the room or if the person won't look directly into the leader's eyes, then there is obviously some problem or deep-seeded secret. It could be that the person seeking employment is lying about some-thing, or he or she is just plain embarrassed to be in the posi-tion of asking for a job. The leader will especially watch the applicant's hands. Are the fingers steady and relaxed, or are they nervously grasping things? Light shaking or sweating hands could mean a health problem, ordinary nervousness, or that the person is not telling the truth about something. Body movements tell similar things, so the leader will look for any twitching, restlessness, or the continual crossing of legs and/or arms. The leader, using his people skills, will in time find out the truth rather than making a quick judgment and possibly missing out on hiring a potential all-star.

Remember, the master leader has to observe everything and not hire just a solid resume or an attractive face. The leader's company depends on winners, and the applicant had better be good enough to depend on. Now, what if an applicant is so smooth and such a good actor that they are hiding the telltale signs of trouble? Well, one shouldn't worry, all leaders make hiring mistakes. Besides, if that actor did such a great job covering up inexperience, bad habits, or health issues, then no one should be surprised if he (with time and coaching) doesn't act his way into the spotlight and become a beacon for all who want to start over.

....

"How a person expresses himself tells all."

HELEN MILLER, BOSTON, MA

....

3. <u>Run a background check</u>: Trust but verify. Always run a background check on your potential employees. Even if a leader has the gut feeling to hire someone on the spot, they should always allow extra time to run a check. This one important practice could save the leader and his company a lot of unforeseen problems. The extra effort that goes into this background check is more than worth it in many ways. For instance, the applicant being interviewed might have a warrant out for his arrest in another state, or he might have just gotten fired from another job for financial or personal misconduct, or he could be a professional con man, jumping from company to company.

   These kinds of problems can be eliminated before they begin if known about in advance of the actual hiring. The master leader's responsibility is to provide a safe environment with a successful, powerful, and enthusiastic team. This goal is impossible to reach if even one of the staff members proves to be a trouble maker, phony, or embarrassment. The leader knows that he's not a doctor, psychiatrist, or minister who can professionally reform a hardened bad apple. The leader has enough molding and coaching to do with his healthy new recruits with clean or forgiven backgrounds. He can't afford to extend himself and spend the company's time and money on some problematic and/or habitual prospect. A leader might not (using good judgment) fire an employee when discovering some flaw that would have prevented the employee's hiring in the first place. Because once the leader/employee relationship is established, the master leader has a professional obligation to help, if possible, the troubled employee. If a leader lets a genuine talent with a troubled background walk out the firm's door without offering any help or encouragement, then the leader involved is shortsighted, selfish, mean, and a little paranoid.

"To be liked is one thing, to be respected is another."

RAY COTTABARREN, MINNEAPOLIS, MN

4. <u>Look for that special spirit</u>: Leaders learn to listen to the tone of voice and watch the eyes of applicants when interviewing them to pick up that special spirit of self-confidence. When a leader is interviewing a person for a sales position, that person's sales talents will clearly be shown. The leader should make mental notes during the interview, remembering the stronger qualities, and writing them down after the meeting is over. The leader must try to know exactly where this or that person could or couldn't fit into his overall sales force or office staff. If the interviewed applicant or salesperson is burnt out, having lost all of his competitive spirit (due to all kinds of reasons), it will definitely show in the facial expressions, the eyes, and the voice. A leader has to judge if such a person has any glowing coals left that might be stirred back into a full-fledged fire. A veteran staff person or salesperson often has the skills and experience to be worth some extra effort on the part of the leader. If the master leader feels that the applicant's coals are ashen and cold, then he will not take on even the most

experienced person. Such a spiritually frigid human can, and most likely will, throw cold water on the flames of the other office members.

5. <u>See whether the applicant has determination</u>: Check for the prospective applicant's drive and determination by noting how much the person wants the job. There are three simple steps that a master leader can take to find out: First, tell the interviewee that he's probably not strong enough to be on the staff or sales team being assembled. Tell him that the whole sales force will be made up of only power hitters and that he just doesn't seem to have the right track record to qualify. After making this statement, the master leader should just sit back and let the person try to sell himself. The leader will then see firsthand if the prospect is a quitter or a fighter who really wants and deserves the job.

   Second, the master leader can try the applicant's patience and perseverance with planned and programmed delays. The leader will first tell the person to come back to the office the next day to complete the interview and evaluation process. If and when the applicant shows up, the leader should tact-fully put the appointment off for another day, making it two delays in a row. If the person shows up on the third day and arrives with the same first-day fire, excitement, and determi-nation, then the leader (if everything else looks good) should hire him.

   Third, the leader should tell the prospective employee that he will only be used on a trial basis until he proves himself (a probation period, if you will). The leader should express some light doubt that the person will successfully pass this trial period and make it to the team. The leader should even act like the offer of a probationary position was a generous and rare gesture on his part. If the person still wants the job on these terms, expresses gratitude for the opportunity, and shows confidence that the trial period will prove his or her worth, then if everything else about the candidate checks out positive, the leader should stand up, shake the person's hand,

and hire him on the spot. The truth is, the leader needs people with a high level of determination and tenacity, and the only way to measure these qualities in a short period of time is with the sometimes painful and frustrating litmus test of the interview methods just described.

....

"If words don't match actions, them I'm resorted to questions."

RANDELL MAXFIELD, MEMPHIS, TN

....

6. <u>See whether the applicant can take criticism</u>: If the applicant cannot take constructive criticism, then he is too temperamental for a professional staff and/or sales team where egos and competition are very visible and important. Every good staff employee and professional salesperson thinks of themselves as God's gift to the business world.

    (**Note:** All great people can learn humility if the lesson comes from a master leader who is respected and shows respect towards others.)

    The easiest way for a leader to see if any applicant is overly sensitive about constructive criticism is right up front, at the initial hiring interview, by addressing their attire. For example, the leader might start off by telling a prospect who is wearing a lot of jewelry that he doesn't want his people to be overly ostentatious. Or, the leader might politely inform the applicant that cowboy boots are not allowed to be worn during work hours. If the person takes issue with these criticisms or expresses resentment at being told what to wear, then the leader knows not to hire him. If the prospect is negative or combative in any small issue, like proper attire, then he will surely be as resistant or even worse to larger issues of corporate policy down the road. The leader has to maintain control, and he has to establish it from the very start, even if he's personally rather partial to cowboy boots. Regardless what an applicant is wearing, its paramount that the leader establishes if the applicant can effectively deal with criticism?

7. <u>See whether the applicant believes in himself</u>: No matter how
    much motivation skill the master leader can muster to get the
    best out of their employee, one must start out with a subject
    who has some measure of confidence in his or her abilities.
    The leader can't always find out in one or two interviews if the
    applicant truly believes in himself or herself. But a leader can
    get a pretty good idea about the person by asking the follow-
    ing questions:

    A. What are your goals in life? (Find out what is it that he's
        really working towards. Almost any answer the leader
        receives will suffice if it is spoken without hesitation and
        conviction.)

    B. Why do you want to come to work for this company and
        not another company who might be the competition?
        (See if he is just floundering relentlessly or trying to drive
        his career forward.)

    C. Why do you believe in yourself? (Ask this directly and
        unexpectedly. As vague and probing as this question is, it
        will be quite interesting and instructive to see if the per-
        son responds with confident humor or serious panic. If the
        applicant believes in himself, he will undoubtedly be spir-
        ited and bold in his statements and answer.)

    Keep in mind, reader, the average prospect is not used
    to this kind of direct, personal questioning and caring from
    a seasoned master leader and will more than likely let his
    guard down. When that happens, the leader can have a five
    minute heart-to-heart talk with the applicant, and that short
    conversation will be worth a lot more than an hour of guarded
    responses.
    These example questions are extremely important for the
    leader to gauge and identify for themselves the confidence level
    of the prospective employee. The leader asks these questions

to comprehend if someone has the fire and potential to make it on a successful sales or office team. If for any reason that belief in oneself has been tarnished, worn down, or lost over a period of time, the master leader has to make a decision whether to attempt a rescue or not.

"Skepticism should be beneath me, but too many times it's not."

WAYNE BURNS, CLEARWATER, FL

8. <u>See whether the applicant has any addiction problems</u>: This is a sad subject to discuss, but with today's statistics and problems, a master leader owes it to his company and fellow employees to find out if a prospect has an alcohol or drug problem. An outright hardcore alcoholic or drug user won't be showing up for an interview, so the master leader has to be smart enough and perceptive enough to pick out the careful but habitual abuser who may seem high powered and confident on the outside. This kind of troubled person is an accident just waiting to happen. Reader, in today's fast and furious world of business, whether embracing opportunity or whispering uncertainty, the habitual abuser is very likely to be among the top prospects. The applicant with a problem will not be telling the truth on this subject, so it is totally up to the leader's instincts and people skills to discover any symptoms and tactfully discuss the matter. When the leader asks the prospect if he has a bit of a problem, he had better ask in a genuinely caring manner. With the help of God and the services of a good counselor, a talented but tortured soul can, in time, turn around and become a miraculous individual, a person everyone can look up to, because somewhere along the line, a master leader courageously believed in them. Most addictions can be unveiled by looking at gaps or inconsistencies in employment. If things don't seem to quit add up, you might just know the answer.

9. <u>See whether the prospect is honest</u>: How can a master leader find out if a prospect is honest? The truth is, it's nearly impossible. The leader can run, as stated before, background checks, make inquiries, talk to others, or a number of other things, but to really know if someone is honest day in and day out is a difficult task. Even if the applicant was a swindler or embezzler in the past, people can change. Dishonest people have become good, honest citizens, and honest people have become crooks. The leader cannot protect himself or his company 100 percent on this matter, and he is sure to get burned every once in a while. The master leader has to remember to stick to honest rules and values, always leading his staff and sales team as the prime example of fairness and trustworthiness. The leader knows, by being true to his word and his principles, in the long run, his good and reliable employees will far outnumber any dishonest ones.

10. <u>Look for loyalty and dedication</u>: If a job candidate has moved around from one company or dealership to another, one can assume that the prospect has little if any capacity for team loyalty. If a prospect has changed schools, addresses, or states over and over again, then the leader should think seriously before investing too much time or effort. The person being interviewed is more of a vagabond than a stable company employee or associate. The only way leaders foster true loyalty and dedication from employees is by first showing loyalty and dedication to employees. Staff members and salespeople must know that their leader will stand with them when they need him. After having been honorably led by example, employees will generally go out of their way to stay loyal to their leader and to their firm. Most, if not all, employees want to be part of a truly professional winning team that they can look back on (in the years to come) and think, "I was an important member of that powerful force." Employees know that to have a top caliber sale force or office staff, loyalty and teamwork are the key factors to make it all work. Nothing succeeds like success, and often that first positive quarterly report begins to push

everyone closer together as a can-do unit. Inevitably, new cohesion focuses in their leader, and the company comes to acknowledge the orchestrator of their success was, from the beginning, the master leader.

2. KEEPING TABS ON EMPLOYEES (SETTING DOWN THE RULES)

"I observe, listen, and identify then draw a general assessment on most people I meet."

RON SALTER, OMAHA, NE

Master leaders (in general) have all of their staff and salespeople sign a standardized statement that lists all of the rules governing the office, the sales and operation, and firm. These rules of conduct should be written in simple and understandable language. This statement should basically list the dos and don'ts to be followed by everyone in the firm. These rules should contain basic cardinal regulations, making it perfectly clear what form of business and personal conduct are not tolerated around the office, including all consequences. This list of rules is invaluable. When someone breaks one of these orders, all the leader has to do is present the employee this signed document from their information file. It is then up to the leader to decide what to do next. At least the employee who, when hired, freely signed the statement now knows that he doesn't have any defense and that his job security is in the hands of the leader. Firings or even severe reprimands aren't easy to administer. But, by showing the signed agreement to the employee, the leader keeps complete control of the situation.

3. STICK BY THE RULES

The master leader has to stick by their operating and conduct rules for the company, and cannot be wishy-washy in executing the penalties for employees who break those rules. If found guilty of misbehavior themselves, the leader will call a meeting and openly confess, apologize, and resign. He or she can then proceed to walk away from the firm with some degree of dignity. The chances are pretty good that the employees and the company owners will ask the leader to reconsider if, of course, the infraction was not too severe. A master leader can turn a potential disaster into a show of integrity by demonstrating to everyone in the company that they were ready to pay the ultimate price for breaking their own rules.

A master leader has to be as fair, but as firm, as a good army general. They cannot make exceptions or bend the office rules to fit a particular situation. The leader is not running a popularity contest; they are running a professional company and/or sales force that has a life and spirit of its own. The leaders job is to keep the entire office team operating together as a confident and prosperous group.

(**Note:** Any preferences, in terms of underserved bonuses, feeding special customers to certain salespeople, or any other like favors that are shown to an employee will only poison and eventually destroy the entire office staff in the long run.) Again, the leader who sets down the rules of conduct had better follow them to the letter himself. If there are changes to be made in any rules, as circumstances dictate, then the leader has to enact the changes openly and above board.

> *"Denying a reasonable person an opportunity is turning my back on faith and possibility."*
>
> DARI CARSLON, ALEXANDRIA, VA

4. EMPLOYEES WITH FINANCIAL PROBLEMS

If a deserving and loyal employee needs some extra financial help, the master will get involved. It is emotionally and financially taxing for a leader to commit oneself to an employee in this dilemma, but can be another significant means for a leader to win undying loyalty. Helping someone out with personal finance doesn't have to mean floating them a several thousand dollar loan or paying overdue rent or dental bills. It does mean getting involved, sometimes by helping the employee become financially organized and fiscally responsible. Keep in mind that dealing with everyday business transactions does not give an employee a facility with personal financial details, so many of them (the employees) greatly appreciate a leader who can take the time to sit down with them and work out (on paper) a financial game plan. Once the leader has stepped in to be the employee's personal banker, or advisor, or accountant, the leader should follow through with periodic checks.

By going the extra mile for an employee, the master leader accomplishes two very important goals. First, he gets the troubled employee back into a positive frame of mind, freeing him from the kind of pressures or uncertainties that would and could hamper his career and productivity. Secondly, the leader has now involved himself right into the employee's personal life. He (the leader) has practically become a big brother or father figure where judgment and directives are sure to be respected and followed.

There is a tremendous amount of positive impact when an employee begins telling his peers what a great person the leader is, how much the leader really cares, and how much he knows about managing money.

5. HAVE REGULAR COMPANY PARTIES

The master leader should have regular company parties to relieve tensions and keep the team spirit alive and elevated. Well done get-togethers keep company excitement thriving. The leader also uses parties to get to know his people and their families better. He can observe his employee's actions and see which ones drink too much, get too loud and rambunctious, or loses control. It is often in such an informal environment that an employee will (for the first time) approach the leader to discuss some problem that would never come up in the setting of the leader's corporate office.

Employees can let their hair and guard down at an office party or outing, but the master leader cannot allow himself to get carried away. He has to always maintain control and set a good example for others. Remember, everyone is always watching the leader whether it's for good reasons or bad. The leader, as always, has to act his role even if it's a difficult task; he's the leader and has no choice.

....

"If a leader expects to be the best of his people,
then he has to give his people the best."

Don Spicer, Chicago, IL

....

6. Show Respect, Receive Respect

Even though a master leader keeps tabs on his employees, he never forgets to show everyone genuine trust and respect. Respect gains respect. Great leaders never need to state their titles because their people know them and what they stand for.

The leader, above all else, takes the time to listen to his employee's problems, ideas, and suggestions. It can't be stated enough that the secret to a successful company is to have each employee feel comfortable, safe, appreciated, and loved. Every person should feel that he or she has a say in company matters and can apply initiative to help spark progress and increase production and/or sales.

A leader will proudly announce at a meeting that a new plan or approach suggested and designed by Mr. or Mrs. employee will be put into effect immediately. This kind of public acknowledgement by the leader makes them feel important and involved, giving them the excitement to inspire every co-worker around them. This positive ripple effect does nothing but boost morale, cooperation, and friendship, three pretty powerful factors that cannot be overlooked or ignored.

Respect also means that an employee who isn't doing well (for whatever reason) will be offered extra training, extra attention, and extra caring, rather than a dressing down. When an employee makes a mistake, his leader's kindness and respect allow the mistake to be forgiven and forgotten. The master leader understands that ultimate success lies in the hearts and minds of his people, and the quicker they know that he respects them, the quicker he in turn will receive loyalty, making him (the leader) feel humble but powerful enough to conquer all.

"To motivate an employee, assign him an exclusively designed task."

AARON HOWELL, SAVANNAH, GA

7. WHAT THE MASTER LEADER MUST KNOW ABOUT EMPLOYEES AND SALESPEOPLE

1. Most successful employees, and all salespeople, think they are the best in the world at what they do. The master leader had better get used to the fact that all good and successful people have large and sensitive egos. This is especially true for salespeople because they are professional optimists and persuaders; their job is selling people their products day after day. When a salesperson becomes a top closer, he or she believes they can sell anyone and make them see things their way. In fact, they begin to think they have all the answers and their leader should also be enamored with their flashes of charm and offers of wisdom. All master leaders appreciate and understand the confidence behind the inflated egos. It's a quality that helps keep the company number one and a quality that keeps the leader working long hours.

2. Master leaders must also be aware of a super salesperson's propensity to exaggerate. All salespeople are actors, and they like to paint their presentations with the brightest of colors. Now, these embellishments and puffing habits are just that, habits. The leader will, to some degree, put up with this communication practice, learning in time to distinguish between the real and the almost real when dealing with his salespeople. A true leader doesn't panic, therefore, when informed

about a "terrible misuse of company assets" or a "vicious fight between salespeople over the weekend"; it was most likely someone only misusing a few dollars' worth of stamps, and two salespeople had only sparred verbally. The leader will calmly go about confirming the information rather than rushing in to make a mountain out of a molehill or reacting with a knee-jerk outburst.

3. There are always some employees in the company who think they can do a better job of leading others than their own boss. All good employees and salespeople feel deep down in their hearts that they could be super master leaders if only given the chance. This intuitive feeling might prove to be true in some cases, but a leader with a sizable ego of his own is not likely to appreciate some self-appointed assistant leader. The leader realizes that even the loudest, most vociferous employee is not threatening his position of authority. He is merely acting out his managerial fantasies. If a leader's top employees didn't feel like dominating a meeting every once in a while, a true leader would think that there is something seriously wrong with staff. It's good to have employees who don't always agree with their leader.

   The master leader will (as stated before) always take the time to listen to his teams criticism or suggestions, hoping to learn something new that will help overall production.

   Note: Sometimes a leader will go along with a questionable suggestion from an employee just to show flexibility. Instead of an I-told-you-so speech after the suggestion fails, the leader will tactfully remind the employee that he did not think much of the proposal from the start. The leader should go on to say that he implemented the proposal nonetheless because he does think the world of the employee. Thus softly humbled, the staff employee with the suggestion or proposal is now, more than ever, ready and willing to be led by the wisdom and experience of the fair-minded leader. Any ego-crazed leader who has stocked his company and/or sales team with yes-men who always agree with him or people who fear him because of his dictatorial style will always have an office staff and sales force that will not produce at their best. The smart leader knows how to step back just enough for innovation and creativity without fully withdrawing and leaving a vacuum for undirected ideas and anarchy.

....

"Deadlines have the ability to eliminate slackers."

MARION ROTH, TOPEKA, KS

....

4. Many employees and salespeople are as lazy as their leader allows. Sure, the average employee will produce, work, and sell, but getting everyone motivated to do their very best without great leadership is nearly impossible. The leader understands the natural tendency to coast if possible, so he has to push, pry, cheer, pull, threaten, and encourage every day. The leader, by example, shows everyone in his company that hard work pays off and that payoff is more than monetary, it's life changing.

In general, master leaders know that their employees are only human. Some might have self-destructive thoughts and habits, some might think no boss is fair, or they might even misinterpret an errand, like having to go to the post office for the company, as a demeaning "punishment exercise" planned by their leader. At times, a leader feels that he's dealing with a group of children instead of adults. In truth, the leader must have the patience and understanding of a parent. The leader will also develop the discipline of a parent, seeing his people through all kinds of emotional rough spots while "raising" them to be highly productive employees who make a very important part of the entire winning team. The leader uses first names, acknowledges everyone, participates in personal conversations, and when invited, laughs, cries, and prays with folks as necessary. Simply put, how the leader begins and ends his day is the exact way his colleagues, subordinates, support staff, and sales force will start and end their day. This statement might sound too simple, but the leader knows for a fact "when love and respect are in the air, then success for everyone is everywhere."

....

"Your future depends on today."

BRENT KELLINGER, CHARLOTTE, NC

....

4.

Giving Meetings

CHAPTER 4

PREPARING EMPLOYEES
AND SALESPEOPLE

The primary objective for meetings, whether the all-important staff, employee, or sales meeting, is to establish control. Without power and direction flowing from the leader's podium, the master leader will never achieve the enthusiasm needed for business success. No matter how effective the leader is in personal one-on-ones, he uses business meetings to project his leadership to the collective group by making them a stage for his strong and focused will. If the meeting's sole purpose is to distribute company information such as inventory or sales percentages, the leader uses the dramatic occasion to spell out significant trends, warnings, or optimistic predictions. No pile of memos written by a competent bureaucrat can create the excitement and aura of influence that a master leader projects at his rallies.

The leader first establishes control over his employees by insisting everyone be on time. Furthermore, the leader establishes his position at these meetings by demanding (in a tactful manner) and getting everyone's attention. All leaders, with their individual styles, will conduct their assemblage differently, some leaders prefer classrooms, teams, or even group war councils, but in none of these get-togethers will any employee be caught catching up on his sleep. Beyond the regular roll call, a leader knows how to engage his employees by calling on his charges to respond to specific questions and remarks. A full range of effects, from visual aids to jokes, is utilized by the leader to keep everyone on the edge of their seats.

Again, because this is very important, the primary way that a master leader controls the energy and pace of his company's employees is by having regular meetings at a set hour. Never forget that the tempo of a meeting orchestrates the working rhythm for the entire company. General meetings are to a corporation what halftimes are to basketball teams, huddles are to football teams, and regroupings are to field generals.

....

"Just like in a track meet, meetings establish a fair and equal starting line."

ROBERT ERICKSON, TAMPA, FL

....

1. SEVEN IMPORTANT REASONS FOR MEETINGS

1. <u>Control</u>: The deputy of control is discipline. The leader demands that his employee meetings be at a certain time, specific location, and with full office dress code in effect. Before conduct-

ing the meeting himself, the leader should involve others by assigning various duties. These might include:

A. Taking attendance

B. Reading the minutes of the last meeting

C. Recording the minutes of the current meeting

D. Handing out relevant company information

E. Seeing that there are adequate chairs in the meeting room, the podium is set up correctly, etc.

Note: Early mornings are the best time for general meetings and/or sales meetings because that is when everyone is alert. It's difficult to exercise control over high-powered salespeople and employees when their minds and bodies are worn out from a hard day's work.

2. Motivate: Never forget that employees can't produce and salespeople can't sell if they are not excited and enthused about themselves and their product. In other words, they have to be constantly motivated, a primary job responsibility of the master leader. The leader uses his employee and sales meetings as the principle vehicles for creating excitement. Once again, no matter how good a coach the leader is to individuals, his meetings are the only organized gatherings that occur regularly where the total population of the company can sit down together and focus in a spirited, unified way toward the same objectives. Any office staff and/or sales force that's operating in different emotional directions without common cause or purpose will eventually deplete itself of energy and self-destruct. Individual awards, spiffs (a type of performance perk) bonuses, prizes, or trophies can keep some employees motivated some of the time, but only energetic, truthful, and well-informed meetings will keep everyone positive and motivated all the time.

The master leader should use his company meetings like a political rally or a sports halftime show, creating a stimulating environment where team spirit can passionately concentrate on particular company goals.

....

"The power that ignites enthusiasm is knowledge."

JAN JANOWSKI, ANN ARBOR, MI

....

3. Educate: Company meetings should also be learning experiences for all employees. The leader must keep his people up to date on any sales and general technical developments related to the organization's product line. The leader constantly teaches his staff and sales force new methods, ideas, and techniques. Plus he engages all employees all year long by charting sales and production progress. The master leader is a professional educator who never allows his instructional sessions to become dull or overly complex. By instinct or by training, a leader knows how to vary his pitch and tone while making eye contact with all, keeping all those involved on their toes.

4. Set specific goals: Company meetings are the perfect venue for leaders to let employees know precisely what is expected of them. In these meetings, leaders have to voice their exact goals or figures (loud and clear) so their employees can see for themselves if they have reached their goals or have fallen short of company expectations.

    A realistic game plan must be drawn up for employees that involves projections over several months. If a leader doesn't have a predetermined plan with a beginning, middle, and end, then he might as well try to win a regatta in a sleek boat without the use of a rudder. Don't forget, you can't tell someone where the first and tenth line is if you don't know yourself. Master leaders let their people understand the overall marketing scheme and objectives so that everyone involved has a clear and common vision of where they need to be headed to get the job done. With specific goals in mind, a struggling employee can be motivated to catch up and an overachiever can feel confident in his progress and/or production.

5. Reward: Imagine if an all-American football player made a touchdown with all of his teammates and eighty thousand fans were watching and not one single person cheered, booed, or applauded. That star athlete would walk off the field and into the locker room, take off his pads, get dressed in street clothes, and never play the game again. It doesn't matter if it's a professional ball club, an army of a million men and women, or a sales team of only ten people. When someone performs well, that person wants, needs, and expects to be acknowledged. If prolific sales go unrecognized, even a veteran salesperson will pack his bags and go elsewhere. Meetings are the ideal forum for giving awards and other team and individual recognition. Everyone can get excited by the team's success brought on by a star employee's achievements.

Even a quiet, introverted employee, when recognized for good work, will be genuinely honored by the group's attention and will be more inclined to give tips and friendly advice to colleagues with whom he might have previously felt competitive or distant. Of course, attention can get addictive, but the leader knows which egos to feed and how much encouragement each employee needs to keep overall company achievement levels at their peak.

- When to give bonuses:
  Question: When should a master leader give out bonuses and other rewards to his employees?
  Answer: At every opportunity. The reward system is an important shot in the arm to any office staff or sales force. It shows employees that the leader not only notices a job well done but also appreciates it.
  Question: Won't bonuses to individuals cause jealousy and resentment?
  Answer: Who cares? Competition is the heartbeat of success. Given in the right spirit, a bonus to an individual will only spur others on to greater efforts. No one will accuse the employee of being the leader's "pet" when reports of his territory's success are presented at a company meeting for all to see and emulate.

It is a good policy to release positive statistics every once in a while and then throw some surprise bonuses or spiffs to everyone involved in the project. These unexpected envelopes of recognition make it feel like Christmas in July. Suddenly, everyone in the office is gushing with enthusiasm and pride. This excitement is immediately passed along to others, or customers, which in turn produces a sudden surge in sales or public relations, an ingenious effect completely orchestrated by the master leader.

What goes around comes around. Any investment in bonuses to the employees will come back to the firm twofold in sales revenues. Those leaders who don't hand out much verbal praise know that these bonuses speak a lot louder than words.

"Instant gratitude and satisfaction are powerful factors in the human subconscious."

DR. LEE KYLE, SAN JOSE, CA

Special Note: Some master leaders, when giving a morning sales meeting, will hand out spiffs to every salesperson before they even meet their customers. The understanding is this: if a salesperson sells his customer, then he gets to keep the spiff. If he goes all day and doesn't sell anyone, then at the end of the day he has to give the spiff back. The power of this idea is simple. The salespeople have spiff money in their pocket in the morning and will sell their hearts out all day to keep that money.

6. Inform: The company meeting is the place to let everyone know what is going on, why it is going on, and how it is going. Master leaders, no matter how busy they are, have the ability to explain procedures and give directives effectively and concisely, letting all of the employees and sales force in on any and all news. Every employee should come out of a meeting feeling like they know everything relevant about their company, their product, the competition, and all developing trends.

Before the sales force or staff hear any of the competition's new financing or rebate campaigns and begin to wonder what effect they will have on their company, the leader will inform them first of the new development and present several ways to counterattack.

Somehow the leader makes information that is familiar to veteran employees seem fresh and compelling, as if the listeners were rookies all over again. The master leader keeps everyone attentive by asking questions, seeking suggestions, and looking for all to not only represent the company but understand the company and thus creating a true family feeling.

7. Regroup: Why does every competitive sports team have a halftime, time out, or between period breaks? Why, for that matter, do army generals hold war councils in the heat of battle? The answer is that in sports, war, and business, the strategies of the opponents are constantly shifting. A master leader too can feel that the opposition has changed to a full-court press, a two-minute drill, or a full-frontal assault.

    The office staff and sales force cannot operate on past momentum when the opposition has made extreme offensive or defensive moves. The leader must regroup, realign, and readjust the company team's movements. A team meeting allows the leader and employees to analyze the competition's thinking and coordinate an effective response. A master leader, like a good coach, will involve everyone in his game plan, making sure the whole force is on the same page in his playbook for the upcoming sales or manufacturing period/quarter. To recap: Keep in mind, reader, the primary way a master leader controls the energy and pace of his employees is by having regular meetings at a set hour. It cannot be stated strongly enough how important regular meetings are to the working rhythm of any professional company staff. Company meetings educate and motivate employees in three general ways:

    A. They bring the whole working force together, allowing it to regroup and reacquaint as a unified team.

B. They allow the employees and leader to rethink strategies and make any necessary adjustments in tactics to new marketing developments in the field.

C. They bring employees back to their inspirational leader, which allows them to concentrate on newly crystallized goals that rejuvenate and keep some from burning out. As if everyone has had a tune-up, the employees should exit a meeting all souped-up and energized about their company.

"I had to ask questions, explore, fail, and depend on faith to find my calling."

ALLEN HARPER, FORT WORTH, TX

2. HOW A MASTER LEADER ACQUIRES THE SELF-IGNITING LEADERSHIP ELEMENT

Reader, this very important topic is placed in this part of the book because you should, by now, have a pretty good understanding of what a master leader is and what he or she does. The secret to leadership is not only being courageous and dedicated to a cause but having the great ability to look inside oneself and create a belief, a spirit if you will, that no person or thing can extinguish. This belief, this seed of possibilities, comes to all who truly search for it with faith and humility. Within everyone a greatness waits to be released. Far too many people are afraid of their own potential; they are scared that the weight of responsibility will destroy or humiliate. Nonsense. The world needs leaders who encourage and help others. People need to see the torch flame of power and promise held high by the brave souls who are willing to give all so others can follow in safety. Leaders are rare but, as the history of man shows, needed. If any person is scared, or doubts their calling, questions their talents or skills, then let them wait in a solitary room of darkness until another opens the door toward the light and says, "I too was afraid until I took the first step toward an honorable tomorrow and found I was stronger than I thought."

Self-Igniting Leadership Element simply means the ability a person possesses to motivate and encourage oneself without any external help.

This special and unique ability is found in the makeup of 95 percent of all genuine master leaders worldwide. How this leadership element is acquired by an individual is an interesting subject. First of all, every human being, no matter where he or she was born or under what conditions, possesses at least one special talent, skill, viewpoint, or ability that can be used to the benefit of all. Secondly, this matchless gift is more than sufficient to make an individual prosperous. Whether a young person is brought up in a positive or negative atmosphere, he needs to seek and surround himself with people who encourage dreams and curiosity—factors positive thoughts feed on. Then, in time, his special skill will surface and the young person can continue to cultivate that gift.

Most people who don't develop their gifts, who don't enjoy the fruits of their inborn talents, have not yet discovered their gifts. When a career and a true talent come together, this partnership grows through courage and confidence from an ember to a great fire that can warm those who come near. In other words, the leader is the person who has the self-confidence (an inner power) to leader other people through difficult situations and to get salespeople to demonstrate sales excellence in all the types of situations. Again, true leaders are the individuals who have discovered, nurtured, and developed their special talents.

Note: Money shouldn't be the career criterion for a leader. The kinds of people who become leaders know instinctively that financial success will follow if they stay true to themselves.

3. How to Motivate Employees

Most, if not all, employees need to be motivated and encouraged and have their self-confidence bolstered. When a master leader confirms those ego-flattering things that most employees privately feel about themselves, then something magical suddenly happens. A positive power is ignited in the employee, causing a true sense of excitement and enthusiasm. The leader knows just how to tease an employee's ego, and in turn that positive turns into greater work habits and productivity.

"Replace agony with humor, and distance all controversy."

SANDRA GUTHRIE, WHITE PLAINS, NY

WORKING ON THE EMPLOYEE'S EGO

The master leader can motivate an employee by just pulling him aside, looking him straight in the eye, and saying in the most sincere way, "Mr. Employee, out of the whole office staff, you are the only one I can depend on day after day." Immediately after delivering this adrenaline shot to the ego, the leader should firmly shake the employee's hand and walk away without saying another word. This little tactic takes seconds, and it works miracles. All employees have egos, and the leader uses this power to his company's advantage.

For example, the leader could make a proud, boastful, and sometimes arrogant employee a team captain, designating him to show the ropes to a new person. By giving the proud ego-charged employee some responsibility, the leader not only gains control of the know-it-all employee but also pushes him into the spotlight where he has to produce to earn his ego-trumpeted reputation.

Another emotional tool the leader uses on an employee's ego, if needed, is shame. A leader can shame an employee into action by having a good old heart-to-heart talk. For instance, when an employee needs to be motivated, the leader, instead of giving some "let's go" speech, can tell the employee how disappointed he is in his performance, how he (the leader) depended on him to be a great example for others in the office. All employees, no matter who they are, cannot dismiss this kind of talking-to. Their ego and the emotions that go with the ego are too strong. All the leader has to do after having this heart-to-heart is just sit back and watch wonders happen.

Using Logic

The master leader can use logic to motivate his employees in a number of different ways. For example, he can privately talk to a debt-ridden employee and logically explain to him that the only way to alleviate massive debt is to stop worrying constantly about his budget and concentrate on work. He (the leader) should explain that the answer to all of the employee's problems is to simply increase income by working different hours or, if in sales, sell more and cut down on spending. The leader could help make a budget plan for the employee and encourage the employee to stick it out.

The leader can motivate an employee burdened with personal difficulties (sickness, divorce, financial etc) and turn him around by reminding the employee of his past years with the company and all of his past victories and triumphs. The leader basically transfers all of the employee's emotional problems into the logical realm of statistics, noting deviations and norms. By using logic, the leader knows how to soothe employee problems with mathematical and mechanical proofs, guiding the troubled or worried employee back to a productive path. With logic, the leader creates an emotional safe house in the office. Instead of an employee bringing their personal problems to the office, they look forward to coming to work and checking their emotional baggage at the door.

....

"Temper fear with understanding and concern."

Dan Waters Sr., Charlottesville, VA

....

Using Fear

Most leaders don't like to use the emotional device of fear to motivate employees, but, at times, it's useful and actually needed. Fear and intimidation can be used like cattle prods in either a direct or indirect way. An example of the direct way involves the leader telling an employee (outright) if he doesn't start or keeps refusing to be a team player, then he won't have a job. Or, fear can be used in a more subtle way. For example, the master leader could completely ignore an employee who is producing poorly. This cold shoulder and an occasional icy stare will cause an agonizing burn in the employee's mind, creating doubts, confusion, anxiety, and the real fear of being terminated.

Fear and intimidation can actually work on problem employees, but it has to be used by a leader who: a) knows exactly what he his doing and b) knows his employee's psychological makeup from A to Z. If this kind of controlling tool is misdirected or used to intentionally hurt someone, then the leader should be fired and the persecuted employee given a second chance with a new leader who understands tact and fairness.

4. Teaching Employees and Salespeople About the Company and Its Products

Each and every employee and salesperson has to know all the relevant technical and general financial details about the company and its products to be truly successful. Even information about how this product is manufactured or how public relations play a part can only bolster the entire office and sales staff.

History of the Company
Everyone working in or around the company office ought to know the history of their firm. This knowledge helps employees feel they matter and are an integral cog in the machinery of the company. Even if the company is one hundred years old, the master leader has got to create dynamic spirit among the staff, as though every person in the office were an industry pioneer. The office staff, along with the salespeople, need to understand how the company functions, who makes out the checks, the order of command, the company's international market share, who has what responsibilities, how the company began, and so on. Every single detail that can make an employee feel important and involved ensures a staff that is enthusiastic, proud, and prosperous.

"Customers will not purchase anything that they don't understand."

Vicki Allison, Boulder, CO

General Product Knowledge

The master leader is responsible for making sure all of his employees, including the sales force, know everything possible about the product(s) being offered. Product knowledge creates a united spirit and common bond among all branches of the company. When this positive bond is shared, the advertising division is aware of what the sales force is doing and the manufacturing division knows what the public relations people are working on. Instead of a so-called group ignorance, all divisions and departments more readily respect each other's jobs. Even some self-centered employees may find themselves cheering the success posted by the shipping or manufacturing personnel.

It's very, very important for a company to be successful; everyone involved has to be totally sold on the overall doctrine of the organization and its product. A trip to the manufacturing plant or a presentation reviewing company awards and advertisements can greatly help with employee enthusiasm. And in turn, that fervor will pass on to every customer or person an employee talks to. If, on the other hand, one company staff member doesn't believe in the worth of the company's product, then that lone low grumble can easily echo throughout the firm, undermining the breath and spirit of the whole office. Remember, the leader is always educating his people about his company's product, explaining details, all benefits, and how his product is better overall than the competition's.

The Competition

The master leader must generally inform everyone in his office about the thinking, product lines, and ambitions of his company's competition. Employees are often too busy to gather or learn information concerning their competition, so it's the leader's job to enlighten. There isn't an employee or salesperson alive who wouldn't herald this company more or sell more if they truly understood their competition's product backwards and forwards.

The leader appreciates that most potential customers have shopped around and researched and investigated products they are interested in. They may have attended seminars, seen demonstrations, or, for that matter, taken a product home for a trial period. The potential customer might even be carrying a recent consumer guide or some other literature listing specific product prices and/or financial payment plans from various institutions. If the leader's employees don't know their competition, it's all too easy for some customer to wave this product literature around, in front of everyone, and try to prove some point.

Any employee on the leader's team who thoroughly knows and understands the competition can truly impress the comparison shopper by saying, "Yes, Mr. Customer, I read the same consumer article you did, and if you notice, our company has the highest rate of customer satisfaction." Reader, know the competition but never, never disparage them or be critical. That type of behavior will not be appreciated by the customer, and they simply will not purchase from anyone they don't respect or appreciate

....

"To keep ahead of my competition, I don't have to like them, but I do have to respect them."

TED ROSENTHAL, FT. MYERS, FL

....

5. SEVEN SUPERIOR MEETING TECHNIQUES

Reader, here are seven meeting themes and techniques that a number of master leaders use to control, motivate, and inspire their employees and sales force. These meeting ideas can be modified so they have the right impact on the audience being addressed. The leader uses these meetings to touch everyone emotionally so they not only learn something but walk away feeling good about their job and themselves.

THE PREQUALIFYING A PERSON MEETING

Definition and Purpose:
This is a shock technique meeting. It is deliberately designed to get the absolute attention of every single person in the meeting room,

whether it is attended by twenty people or an audience of a thousand. In this fun and unique meeting, employees and salespeople are taught, in a very realistic way, not to prequalify or prejudge prospects and not to evaluate them as desirable or undesirable people before even saying "hello." This type of meeting can only be executed and delivered if the guest speaker is known but not physically recognized by the audience.

How This Meeting Is Executed and Delivered:
This is definitely a theatrical meeting, one that should be rehearsed to get the timing down. First, the master leader asks a special person to be the guest speaker at one of his regular meetings. This guest speaker can be a writer/author, a doctor of psychology, or a retired military general. All that matters is that the guest speaker's name is well known by the leader's audience.

(**Note:** Again, the audience knows the name of the guest speaker but doesn't know what he looks like.) The second thing that the leader needs is a janitor's pullover jumpsuit along with a long-handled push broom.

Now, before any employees show up for the meeting, the leader should ask his guest speaker to put on the janitor's jumpsuit over his street clothes and try to look and act like a real janitor doing some last minute cleanup work in and around the area of the meeting. As the employees keep filing into the meeting room, the disguised guest speaker pushes his broom. He should act as though he's tired and wants to rest. He should sit down next to a few employees, preferably some of the best-dressed who are just settling into their chairs. Invariably, nearly every employee the "janitor" tries to sit next to will either politely tell him that the seat is already taken by a colleague who is running late or the employee will discreetly move away and find other seats in a different area of the room. In other words, these musical-chair employees tend to think they are too good to sit next to a janitor when they have come to the meeting to listen and discuss "big important business." A meeting they understand will be headlined by a distinguished professional speaker talking about highly complex issues.

The "janitor" should, as the employees are taking their seats, move around the meeting room randomly trying to find a place to sit. After more than several attempts among the well-heeled employees, the "janitor" should quietly go to the back of the meeting room and stand still and unnoticed while the meeting gets started. After a few opening remarks, the master leader (the guest speaker's accomplice) should excitedly introduce the guest speaker. The minute the guest speaker is introduced (while receiving great applause), he should walk crisply down the center aisle with push broom in hand, straight up on stage, and right to the podium.

Without speaking a word (during the stunned silence, pierced with a smattering of low, nervous laughter), the guest speaker should let the broom fall by the podium and take off the janitor's pullover jumpsuit. Slowly, and with grand gestures, the guest speaker should straighten his tie, look directly at the shocked audience, and soberly state: "The reason this company is not doing as good as it could is because a lot of employees and salespeople are in the bad habit of prejudging and prequalifying others. If you would take more time to understand other people, your company could and would be extremely successful." The guest speaker delivers these punch lines that rock the crowd back on their heels. "As a janitor, I tried to get a seat in this very room, but I couldn't. It seems that I wasn't good enough. If any one of you knew that I was the guest speaker, I could have gotten a seat anywhere." Then after offering this powerfully demonstrated point, the guest speaker, with a thank-you nod toward the master leader, should continue on with his prepared talk.

....

"Don't talk at your people, talk with your people."

JEAN BEACHHAM, PHILADELPHIA, PA

....

THE COUNTDOWN-TO-GOAL MEETING

Definition and Purpose:
Time is the enemy. This is the basic theme in the Countdown-to-Goal meeting. The purpose is to set a short-term goal and then have everyone in the office work toward that particular goal. The main

objective here creating an immediate surge in the overall spirit of the entire office staff and/or sales force. The master leader uses this kind of employee meeting to start off a sixty-day contest or to mark the beginning of any important sales deadline. The leader has to keep in mind that he can only use this type of meeting two or three times a year and that each short-term goal has to be just that, short term. Otherwise the salespeople or office personnel will get burned out early and fail in the leader's overall game plan.

This short-range employee contest is wonderfully devised to get everyone giving a 100 percent effort for an eight-week period of time. At the end of the eight weeks, rewards, parties, and congratulations will flow in abundance. Individual winners in the competition will be enthusiastically recognized, but not a single employee should be labeled a loser. Because the contest was successful, and the company has dramatically increased production, everyone should feel as if they've won. For this type of meeting, the leader has to have set rules for the contests and strictly follow them. Some employees who worked hard could easily feel cheated that they did not win in a contest where the supervision and oversight was lax. If any productive employee feels that they lost in a competition due to a popularity game, then their resentment may carry them right out the company's doors and into the waiting arms of the competitive firm.

How This Meeting Is Executed and Delivered:
Without any of the employees knowing and without any advance warning, the master leader (after he has developed all of his plans and knows exactly how his contest will work) should announce in one of this regular morning meetings that starting from that very day and for the next sixty days, there will be an all-out, full-throttle employee contest requiring maximum effort. He should reveal the rules of the contest and the rewards waiting at the end of the sixty-day period. The leader should let it be known that first, second, and third place prizes will be awarded to the employees who demonstrate the highest efficiency performance during that timeframe. The leader should make large and colorful visual charts or graphs to let everyone know exactly where they stand, and he has to announce the progress of everyone each and every day. The leader makes this contest look and

feel like a major horse race. He has to constantly create excitement and encourage enthusiasm.

The reward and/or prizes the leader dangles in front of his employees had better be good ones and have real value. This contest, if done properly, you should anticipate an increase in productivity by at least 10 percent thru the momentum created alone.

....

"Tremendous meetings are given by tremendous people."

P. L. Ostler, Eugene, OR

....

The Positive Approach Meeting (Showing Some Class)

Definition and Purpose:

In a meeting like this, the leader wants to achieve only one goal, and that goal will automatically lead to a super day of production by her employees. The master leader wants their office personnel to feel like royal professionals. She wants to make everyone feel that they are part of one of the strongest office or sales teams ever assembled and that there isn't an office staff anywhere powerful enough to climb on board. In this meeting the leader wants to work on her employees' egos and make them, collectively, feel taller than they have ever felt before. The leader wants everyone to feel so good about themselves that they will stop worrying and whining about their own person problems and only focus on the job that needs to be done that day. She tells her employees how proud she is to be associated with them and how rare it is for so many pros to be on the same team, all at the same time. The leader can really lay it on thick in a meeting like this because everyone only wants to hear more. When praising her employees to this extreme degree, she must keep in mind that she can only use this super-positive approach a few times a quarter. If it is utilized too often, it will lose the effect that was intended.

How This Meeting Is Executed and Delivered:

This employee meeting has to be given the day after a great day of production and never, never after a bad day or it will sound insincere and phony. Right after the roll has been taken, the leader should stand in front of his employees and say something to this effect, "Today I want to tell you all something that I have never before told you as a group. The reason I'm telling you this now is because of something my daughter said to me last night. She asked me how much do I enjoy my job, and after I answered her she asked if I ever told the people I work with how I felt. I thought about that, and it bothered me all night. So, today I want to share my feelings with you. I have been in this business for a long time, as all of you know, and I have been around many of the best office personnel and salespeople in the world at one time or another. But, I want you all to understand something: in all of my professional life, I have never been associated with so many wonderful, caring, and talented people as you. This group that we have here is one of the strongest and most powerful teams that I'll ever have the honor to lead. I love my job, not because of some so-called title or position; I love it because I can work with you, learn from you, and succeed with you. I just wanted to tell you that. Now let's focus, have a great day, and show the world that we have honor and class."

"Never ask an employee to do something you aren't willing to do."

GEORGE LARREMORE, SEATTLE, WA

THE BONUS SURPRISE MEETING

Definition and Purpose:

This meeting is unlike the Countdown-to-Goal meeting because it's only for one day. This meeting has to be an absolute surprise for all employees. It's intended to generate excitement and momentum on the spur of the moment. The master has to be on hand all day long (as he should be anyway) to give this one-day contest the feeling of being official. The leader should know exactly what he wants to accomplish with this challenge and already have the rules written down so everyone can follow them and know what to do. The Bonus Surprise meeting means at the end of the work day (not the next day), the leader will hand out the rewards or bonuses to the employees who win.

If the bonus is monetary, then it's best if the leader hands the winner cash. The reason is simple: cash or gold make an impact. Employees understand cash, silver, or gold a whole lot better than they would a piece of paper with someone's signature on it. Nothing makes employees work harder than to know at the end of a day he or she can spend their reward. Leaders can run little surprise contests like this all year long to keep everyone motivated.

How This Meeting Is Executed and Delivered:

When production and sales are down and some employees are walking around like zombies, then the master leader needs to immediately, if not sooner, do something. To pick his employees up in a hurry, the leader uses the Bonus Surprise meeting. Right after roll call has been taken, the leader should tell his employees something along these lines: "Alright everyone, we all know that our sales and production have been down. They are not near what we've projected them to be. Each one of you, including me, can do a whole lot better, and we all know that. Today we're going to have some fun and laugh at the last few days. So here is what I'm going to do. Starting right after this meeting, everyone who sells, promotes, manufactures, or whatever task is your responsibility, will have the opportunity to draw from this sealed box one slip of paper that will have a dollar amount printed on it. Inside this box there are enough slips for everyone. Now, the dollar amount on each slip of paper starts at twenty dollars and goes up to one thousand dollars. So, at the end of this day, everyone, after cashing in, will have at least twenty dollars extra. To make this interesting, there are three pieces of paper with a thousand marked on it, four slips with five hundred, and ten slips with one hundred, and the rest twenty. These slips of paper will be exchanged for dollars at the end of this day. There is only one catch. If one person is caught (there must be witnesses, one in management and two employees) talking negatively, acting rudely, or just trying to coast through the day without any positive attempt to produce, then no one gets the change to cash in their money slip. If one person lets down the job, we all suffer. Remember, we are a team, and today let's act like the winning team we know we are so everyone has cash. Don't, fellow employees, hurt others who depend on you."

Right after the leader says these things, he should hold up a fistful of hundred dollar bills to let the employees know he has the money in hand.

The leader could add, "Oh, by the way, the people who get the one thousand dollar slips can take tomorrow off. This is a one-shot deal folks, so I hope everyone takes full advantage of it. Now, let's start acting like professionals and make some money."

After the master leader has enthusiastically delivered this little speech, he should ask his assistants to take over and let the employees line up and draw from the box. Don't forget, the master leader always has to head the company's employees in the right direction, and money or gold tend to be a pretty reliable compass. If funds are low, try using extra days off, up-close parking passes and dinners with the leadership team.

....

"Employees enter meetings needing inspiration, wanting promise, and expecting miracles."

BROOKE PATRICKS, OKLAHOMA CITY, OK

....

THE NEGATIVE APPROACH MEETING

Definition and Purpose:

The meeting technique described here uses the power of reverse psychology. This is a meeting conducted by the master leader to make his employees feel a little shameful and embarrassed about their recent poor performance and progress. This meeting (when necessary) is designed to work on the employees' raw "fight back" emotions and turn those irritated emotions into positive and productive ones. The leader who gives this kind of meeting has to be well respected by his employees, or it will never work. The Negative Approach meeting will produce positive results, but it cannot be used more than two days in a row and only a few times throughout the year. Anyone, included hardcore salespeople, can only take so much constructive criticism, and when they have had their fill (when they think their leader is purposely humiliating them), they will rebel and walk out of the meeting, or on some cases, walk away from the company. To deliver a Negative Approach meeting, the leader must know to the letter what he is doing, and he must know just how far he can push his employees. If a leader doesn't know for sure the breaking limits of his people (what they can and can't take), then he should give this type of meeting in a watered-down version. Meaning, highlight the challenged areas and not personify them.

How This Meeting Is Executed and Delivered:

When the master leader's office or sales team has had a week or more of slow ineffective production, this is the kind of tough meeting he can deliver that will produce positive results that very day. Before the leader gives this little leathery talk, he has to stay away from everyone in the office (he can even hide away in his private office with the door locked if necessary) and give the appearance that he is upset. The leader has to provide others the impression that he is very serious and really means business. Warning: (the leader) can't joke around with anyone or join in small talk with any of his employees before he gives the Negative Approach meeting, or it's impact and effect will be totally lost.

Now, when the employees are all seated in the meeting room, the master leader should slowly walk to the front of the group and state: "There is a reason every one of you is here with this company. In fact, I personally went out of my way to hire some of you. If you all remember, when a few of you needed help, I was there, I've stood by you, bailed you out of trouble, and believed in you when no one else would. When this company hired you, it was a given that you were the very best professionals in your field. But, according to our sales and production figures, it looks like that isn't true. The last week or so has been so disappointing that I'm starting to believe I made a personal mistake in depending on you. Today, I need your help. I don't need excuses, I don't need any tears, all I need is for you to be you. The You that I've staked my reputation and future on. Folks, I'm under the gun right now, and I really need a professional performance and not a bunch of people running around with a rookie mentality that I have to oversee and tell them what to do. Today, I need employees who are as good as the ones I have put my money and faith in. So, I'm going back to my office and do my job for you, just like I always have done, and I'll do that job to the very best of my ability. I'm not going to worry about you, and I'm not going to yell. You all expect the best from me, and I'll give it. I, in turn, expect the best from you."

After the leader has made this talk, he should go right back to his office and shut the door. This kind of meeting works wonders, but again, the leader has to deliver it in a very somber and dramatic way.

....

"Gatherings and meetings become rallies through passion."

SCOTT GARCIA, FLAGSTAFF, AZ

....

THE STAND UP FOR MONEY MEETING

Definition and Purpose:
Reader, this type of meeting has been around forever. It's simple, fun to give, and very basic in its message. The reason it's even mentioned in this book is because it works and will always work. Sure, it's elementary and rookie-like, but we would rather include this kind of meeting than completely ignore it. The master leader gives these meetings for one reason only: to illustrate to every employee that one has to physically move to make money. When the leader uses this kind of demonstration on his employees, it will not only get positive results but will be remembered and talked about for a long time to come. The master leader can only use this type of meeting once every nine months. If he uses it more frequently than that, it becomes a joke. Remember, reader, people, as you know, are always impressed with cash or gold, and cash is what this exercise is all about.

How This Meeting Is Executed and Delivered:

Before any employees arrive at the meeting, the master leader has to secretly tape a hundred dollar bill to the underside of every chair that will be used. After he has taped the money where it can't be seen, he opens the meeting room doors so his employees can enter and be seated. Then, acting as though everything is normal, he proceeds with his regular morning meeting. The leader, during his briefing, should only talk about work habits and stress how necessary it is for employees to always be active, moving over their territories, looking for new customers, and searching for new ideas that will improve their performance. Throughout his talk, the leader should explain how movement develops into action and that no one can make a good living by just sitting around dreaming a good life. The leader tells everyone that they have to hustle, explore new avenues, and dare to believe in taking risks if they're ever going to get ahead.

After the leader has delivered this speech, and just before he adjourns the meeting, he should instruct all of his employees to stand up right where they are and turn over their chairs. When the employees discover the money, the leader should say, "Remember folks, to make money you have to get off your rear ends." Boom! The leader has made his point, the employees have an extra hundred dollars, and the spirit of loyalty and gratitude are reinforced. After this type of meeting, the leader will see a very productive day, and he will easily recoup the money he invested. If funds are tight, the use of twenty dollar bills can be just as motivating and drive the same behavior.

....

"Don't expect a miracle if you're not willing to do your part."

SHARON COLVIN, LAS VEGAS, NV

....

THE SHARPEN YOUR AX MEETING

Definition and Purpose:

This is a meeting where the master leader makes a very important point by telling a story. This short story is a great one; it encourages employees to continue learning about their profession. The leader should practice telling this before they deliver it because it's too good to be botched in front of everyone at the meeting. The wonderful effect this tale has on the employees is that it logically gets the leader's point across loud and clear and, at the same time, doesn't really step on anyone's toes. This brief act, which should be incorporated into the overall meeting theme, works. It will be remembered by all employees as making a powerful and fundamental statement. Reader, after the leader has told this moving idea, he should let it soak into his employees' minds for a few seconds, then move on to the rest of his program.

How This Meeting Is Executed and Delivered:

This special story can be told at the very beginning of the meeting or sometime during the meeting, whenever the master leader feels it will have the most impact. Don't forget, this is a story the leader tells if he wants to make a point about how all employees need to constantly study new information concerning their professional field.

The story: "One time there was this young man from Texas who wanted, more than anything, to be a professional lumberjack. Now, this young man was big, strong, and powerful. In fact, he could have played on any professional football team in the country if he was so inclined, but that wasn't in his heart. What he wanted was to move to the great Northwest and become the most famous lumberjack that ever lived. Right after he graduated from college, he packed up his belongings, put them in his pickup truck, and headed northwest. When he finally arrived in the state of Washington, he went directly to a logging camp, entered the main office, and told the foreman, 'I'm from Texas and I've driven all this way to become a great lumberjack, so please just give me a chance.' The foreman thought for a minute and decided, why not? So, he handed the young man an ax and told him to put his gear away in the bunkhouse and get started.

"The young Texan went enthusiastically out into the woods where there were already a hundred other men working, and he started chopping down trees. That very first day the young man (to the astonishment of everyone) single-handedly chopped down 250 trees. That night he went into the chow hall, had a big meal, didn't talk to anyone, and went to bed early. All through the night, he kept thinking to himself, if everyone thinks I'm good, wait until they see me tomorrow. At dawn on the second day, he got up, went out, and worked all by himself for ten straight hours, but this time he only chopped down one hundred trees. Annoyed with himself, but still amazing the other men, he skipped supper entirely and got to bed very early, determined to do a super human job the third day. That third morning he was out in the forest before anyone else, and he worked extra hard the entire day plus some, a total of twelve long hours, but this time he only chopped down six trees. Completely baffled, bewildered, and angry at himself, the young Texas man walked back into the foreman's office and threw his ax on the table, stating, 'That's it, boss. I've had enough. I thought I could be a great lumberjack, but I was wrong. I'm not good enough; I'm going back to Texas to play football!' Then he turned and started out the door. That's when the foreman said, 'Hold it, young man. Remember you told me that first day you wanted to be the greatest lumberjack of all time? Well, you are. You're the most powerful lumberjack we've ever seen around here. Why, you chopped down more trees than ten men put together. You wanted to be great. Well, to the rest of us, you are great. But you've made one little mistake. Every night, after chopping down so many trees, you simply forgot to bring your ax in and have it sharpened.'"

After the leader tells the story, he should then say to his employees, "Everyone, just keep in mind that we all have to sharpen our mental axes every single day if we expect to be the best."

6. MEETING NOTES TO REMEMBER

"I always put the whisperers and rebellious souls in the front row."

DEBORAH SEDGWICK, READING, PA

1. <u>Be on time</u>: There is an old saying, "If you are not ten to fifteen minutes early, then you're late." The master leader's first line of defense in maintaining control is to have every employee

on time for the regular scheduled meetings. The leader must establish a precise time for the daily meeting to start. If an employee is tardy, then he or she is showing a no-respect attitude. Most leaders will actually lock the meeting room door after the meeting begins, not allowing any person in, with the understanding the late person will be put on probation for the rest of the day. In truth, lateness illustrates that an employee does not care. Time, to all leaders, is very important. They ensure that they are prepared for the day long before the day tries to prepare them. If any sales team or office staff is going to thrive, its leader must set the pace and illustrate to all that being timely is a key component to success.

Time and time again, leaders and their employees distinguish themselves from others by having the ability to be ahead of the race and maintain their consistency by never allowing themselves to be late for any appointment or meeting.

2. Enforce the dress code: If a master leader wants a successful sales force or office staff, he had better pay close attention to how everyone looks. It's a fact of life that 80 percent of a person's attitude is determined by how he or she feels about themselves, and if someone feels well dressed, they will act professionally. Or, to put it another way, if someone dresses for success, then they will perform and act successful. If an employee looks unkempt or out of sorts for the morning meeting, the leader will send that person home to change. There is no excuse whatsoever for any employee to look unprofessional.

3. Ban cell phones: When a leader is holding his employee meeting, it has to be absolutely understood by everyone that all phones are to be turned off. The reason for these strict rules is so the master leader can keep control and conduct a serious meeting without any interruptions. Employees have to learn sooner or later, through daily mental exercise, that when the leader talks, everyone listens. The leader has to drill into his people a subconscious awareness that he rules the nest.

Every little sidebar incident the leader tolerates, or lets slide, will only erode his leadership capabilities and the respect he has worked so hard to maintain.

Don't forget, if a leader lets one tiny interruption go by without notice, then that could, and most likely will, pave the way for other things to slide by, thus creating an avalanche that will eventually bury the leader.

4. <u>Don't tell all:</u> It is very important to note that if a leader tells his employees every little thing that is going on in his office (bank business, contract negotiations, meetings with lawyers, company programs for future product development, delicate mergers, or closed-door financial transactions, etc.), then he will lose his job. Every small bit of classified information or restricted communication the leader casually discloses to others will come back (in a big way) to haunt him until he finally quits his job or gets fired. The leader *cannot* tell all things to all people. He has to hold the details of his programs and overall game plans close to the vest. If he lets others in on his secret courses of action or promotions before they are actually carried out, there will always be a person (or a bunch of somebodies) who will try to interfere, derail, or distort his good intentions.

....

"Dream about victory, presume victory, work with diligence, then proclaim victory."

STAN LAPIERRE, GREENVILLE, SC

....

5. Keep it to twenty <u>minutes only:</u> When a leader holds his regularly scheduled meeting longer than twenty or twenty-five minutes, then he's passed right by his employees' maximum time limit for concentrated attention. Most energetic employees are a restless breed, revving to succeed early into each new day. If the leader is long-winded or takes too much time

explaining certain points during his meeting, his audience (no matter how loyal) will get bored and won't pay full attention. Employees in general want energy-charged meetings to help them get stimulated for the day, and the leader can only deliver this magic energy in short, planned, powerful blasts, not in an ongoing and agonizing stream of dialogue.

6. Use the assistant leader: The master leader has got to use his sidekick leader (manager) all of the time and at every meeting. The reason: the assistant helps make the leader look and stay important. The master leader knows that he can't do everything by himself, and his sidekick is there to help. In everyday meetings, the master leader doesn't always have the time to tend to details or so-called trivial matters; it's the assistant leader who loyally organizes and sees that orders are carried out. A good sidekick can take attendance, make inventory adjustments, hand out general company information, or, if need be, tape hundred dollar bills to the bottom of the employees' chairs.

   There are numerous duties that an assistant leader can do, and the master leader should be more than grateful for this true comrade-in-arms.

   Note: Employees like to know that their master leader is thinking about them, so it's very wise for the leader to call roll himself every now and then.

7. Mix employees and managers: When the master leader has managers, team captains, or other assistants in addition to his trusty sidekick, he had better make sure the assistants sit right among the employees. The master leader wants more than anything to create a total team spirit, not one that is divided between employees and managers. If there is such a division where all the managers sit up front at a meeting table, facing the employees, who in turn are facing them, then, believe it or not, a real friction starts to develop. The gap that opens between these two parties will be awful. Team spirit will be divided, and the two parties will slowly start to console and

trust only themselves. There should always be a feeling of helping and caring for each other and the common goal of succeeding together.

....

"The best thing you can show an employee who is a constant pessimist is the door."

MIKE AREVALO, ST. LOUIS, MO

....

8. Explain goals: The master leader has to let all of his employees know what their company's overall goals are. This is the only real way the whole team can collectively visualize the exact same targets and share the same enthusiastic spirit. Without a united front directed towards a common interest, the team is not a force (concentrated energy that creates action) but merely a bunch of individuals frantically going in every direction, bumping and stumbling over each other's paths, hoping in some way to accomplish a miracle.

9. Give recognition: When an employee does an outstanding job, then by all means, give him or her the deserved recognition. Leaders never delay rewarding an employee for an outstanding performance. The leader uses his meetings like an actor uses the stage: to jolt emotions, expand feelings, and applaud character. The leader accomplishes these feats by publicly giving out praise to any employee who deserves it. Reader, if you hand someone a trophy, they will never let it get tarnished.

10. Keep records: It's very important for the master leader to keep minutes of every meeting. The main reason is to protect himself from some unforeseen challenge, problem, or dispute. For instance, if an employee makes a complaint, saying that this or that was going to take place at a certain time and it never came about, then the leader (by having correct records) is well protected. All the leader has to do is refer back to the minutes of the meeting covering the disputed subject. Any

controversy is immediately solved by showing the disgruntled employee precisely what took place and what was said. It is also very important for the leader to keep daily accounts of his sales forces' closing percentages, length of time spent with customers, and any other relevant data so he knows exactly where each individual salesperson stands.

11. Accept that cliques do exist: The master leader has to understand that there will always be cliques (buddies) who stick together no matter what their leader does or says and no matter what the circumstance or situation is. Even if some members of the clique are in management and others are employees, the leader knows friends will be friends. The leader realizes that he shouldn't attempt to break up any of these close-knit groups because he wouldn't succeed, plus he'll be resented by everyone involved in the private club. Cliques are good for companies because within their own inclusive sphere, the members help each other by spurring support, empathy, and encouragement in ways the master leader and outsiders cannot.

   The only thing a leader has to watch out for is intimate groups that continually cause negative thinking within the rank and file. Now, when the leader discovers an incident where a certain group is intentionally trying to cause trouble, he should immediately have a private and diplomatic talk with the group's head person (there will always be a "top dog") and try and get things straightened out. If the top dog is difficult to manage and/or have a civil conversation with, then the master leader should stand straight, look the top dog in the eyes, and fire him on the spot. The leader should make the firing an example to the other clique members. They, in turn, will either shape up or ship out. The leader has to be very strong in these situations or his reputation and his policies will be worth nothing.

"No leader can lead from afar."

RON BAUER, PALM SPRINGS, CA

12. <u>A.M. is the best:</u> The perfect time of day for the master leader to hold his meetings is always in the morning. Why? Because employees are more alert and energetic at that time. The leader's main objective in having an early morning meeting is to get his employees psyched up for the rest of the day. The leader knows if his employees have a productive morning and all spirits are high, then the rest of the day should follow suit. Again, nothing breeds success like success. The leader has to be the employee's alarm clock, morning motivation, bringer of new information, and cheerleader every single day if he wants his company and his people to be triumphant.

13. <u>Stay around:</u> To have a successful company day after day, the master leader must stay around the office. He can't just give a blockbuster employee meeting and then leave the office, expecting his assistants to carry the day. The leader has to be on board. If he has satellite offices, then he will visit them, make his presence known, and do his job.

    The leader is just that: the leader. While he is around his office, or offices, his employees will work. Once he is away, his employees tend to relax and not overly exert themselves. This is a universally known fact: employees have to be watched, pampered, and led. The leader cannot give directions to his people when he isn't there to guide them. Don't forget, employees will only work as hard as their leader works. This is a game changer and every master leader in the world knows it to be true.

    Note: While in and around the company's offices, the master leader has to be highly visible, not hidden behind closed doors in his private office. His employees want to be recognized and greeted, and they can't if their leader is not present or out among them.

....

"Employees who don't want to be saluted are either overly shy or not doing their job."

KEVIN COLE, KNOXVILLE, TN

....

14. <u>Setting Expectations:</u> The master leader understands the stone cold truth that his people will only be as good and as powerful as he is. If a so-called leader is weak, wishy-washy, uncertain of his actions, or unreliable, then his employees will behave the same way. The leader is the only person who has the lone responsibility to make his team of employees successful not only financially but morally as well. The master leader is the pulse of his people, and he can never afford to forget it.

He has to give spirited and educational meetings, keep calm, be in control, be wise, and, behind closed doors, go crazy every once in a while. Needless to say, being a professional leader is not, by any stretch of the imagination, easy. Aside from all the various qualities mentioned in this book, the leader, no matter what, must remain honest, strong, and dependable even when all others have fallen short or retired from exhaustion.

....

"Employee's will rise or fall to their leaders expectations"

JWW & JWP

....

5.

The Master Leader Helps the Sales Team

CHAPTER 5

Reader, we are now going to shift gears and discuss the master leader and their sales force. Previously we have looked at the leader, their staff and office personnel and every so often mentioned the salespeople. But it's time in the leader's overall organizational plan to concentrate on the responsibilities and duties pertaining to their team of salespeople.

The leader not only has to lead and encourage his office employees but also has to direct and oversee the company's sales division. In fact, the leader is a true salesman at heart, and through their busy day, there are times when they will actually help salespeople sell.

If a salesperson wants or needs help in closing a customer, he cannot ask for a better professional closer than the master leader. The leader is smart, fast, wise, alert, knowledgeable, and downright deadly when it comes to closing a customer on their company's product.

A T.O. situation is where the master leader really gets to demonstrate to the employees true sales prowess. The initials "T.O." in sales simply mean "take over" or "turn over." This grand and delicate event takes place when the master leader is called in by one of the salespeople to finalize a sale, wrap up any loose ends, or actually sell a difficult customer.

"When you help, and put another person first, you'll never be last."
JANELL LINDSEY, TULSA, OK

1. THE MASTER LEADER AND THE T.O. SITUATION

Most, if not all, master leaders are great sales closers. They love it (if they have the time) when one of their salespeople comes to them and asks for help in selling (closing) a customer. It's like old times for the leader. No matter how long a master leader has been away from selling his own customers, he never forgets the excitement and the raw positive energy that flows through everyone at the closing table when a customer finally makes the buying decision to purchase the company's product. In truth, it's these well-honed instincts and wonderful memories that spark the leader's enthusiasm when asked to T.O. In a "take over" sales situation, the leader not only gets the chance to sell a customer, but he also gets the chance to show his employees that he is willing to get back into the trenches and work just like everyone else. If, for instance, the leader successfully takes over a difficult customer, then he has accomplished more for team morale than a dozen seminars or sales meetings. No real leader can pass up an opportunity to get into the spotlight and shine every once in a while.

2. WHEN IS THE RIGHT TIME FOR THE MASTER LEADER TO T.O.?

It is very important for the master leader to know exactly when to T.O. If a leader doesn't understand the difference between good timing and bad timing, then he should never try to T.O. Again, a professional "take over," "turn over," or "tactical offense" can only be successful if the leader is a top-notch closer and knows what he is doing. Leaders know that timing and gauging a customer's emotions are everything when it comes to executing a professional T.O.

1. <u>When the salesperson is losing the customer</u>: Since sales are the bottom line for any great company, the master leader doesn't want to wait to tell a salesperson what he might have done differently to save a lost sale. When the leader sees that one of his salespeople is losing a customer's interest and enthusiasm for the product, then he (the leader) has the full right to step in on the sales presentation and give all he's got to save the deal. If the master leader happens to step on his salesperson's toes during this intervention, then that's just too bad. The customer is everything, and if there is any outside chance to satisfy the customer and make a sale, then it's worth the risk of making a salesperson feel temporarily slighted. A true master leader will never silently stand by and watch a valuable customer slip through the fingers of a salesperson who has given up too early in the sales presentation or who has not taken the time to completely and properly explain the product.

   Of course, a leader who bursts into the closing scene should do so with all the charm he can muster. After a T.O., the leader should soothe the involved salesperson's bruised ego by congratulating him on his effort. Then when the salesperson is feeling better about himself, the leader could slip in a few words of advice on how to better handle a similar situation in the future.

"When someone asks for your assistance, treat it like an honor."
EUGENE O'REILLY, PADUCAH, KY

---

2. <u>When a salesperson asks for help</u>: The master leader has a professional responsibility to assist not only his office staff of employees but also his salespeople, and he should be available (when possible) for a T.O. when they need one. The leader has directly, or indirectly, hired and trained his salespeople,

and for him to not follow up when necessary or lend a hand when they need him is nothing short of abandonment.

Now, a leader shouldn't go out of his way to be a meddler. He should strike the right balance by knowing his sales staff and only rush over to a fledgling salesperson when they are visibly losing altitude. All salespeople will do their own closing, but they are sure to produce a lot better knowing that they have a strong and powerful backup system in place if ever needed.

Note: Sometimes a sales team will have a salesperson who has gotten in the habit of calling on the leader to T.O. nearly every one of his customers. This kind of salesperson is only using his boss (the leader) as a crutch. This bad habit only keeps the salesperson as a dependent employee, encroaching on the leader's busy daily schedule. The master leader, in this situation, has the full right to ignore this type of salesperson's distress calls. The leader may want to slowly wean the salesperson away from dependency with increasing unavailability or increasingly early exits from the closing table, which will force the salesperson to learn and execute more of the actual closing process.

3. <u>When the master leader knows the customer</u>: Occasionally a situation arises when the salesperson's customer is a personal friend or acquaintance of the master leader. The leader might also have a referral customer who comes asking for him at his company by way of one of the leader's past customers. When situations like this occur, then it is proper for the leader to take over this customer if he so elects. In fact, the customer might even feel slighted if the friendly, familiar face he came looking for is not willing or available to see him. In these cases, the leader should never (if the customer buys something) take a commission. He should either divide it up as a sales bonus for the whole sales team to share or he should give it to the salesperson who has first-hand contact with the customer.

If, on the other hand, the leader takes the commission himself, it is guaranteed that problems will develop from jealous sales employees. The leader understands if he lines his own pocket first, all will know. Any petty gossip that unfolds from the incident could well escalate into a bunch of nasty and vicious rumors, and the commission, no matter how much its value, will never be worth more than a pile of regret. In times like these, a leader knows that earning respect and avoiding trouble are much more important than acquiring money.

"To restore comprehension, ask the customer how he would describe the product being offered for sale."

JERRY LAMB, DENTON, TX

4. <u>When the salesperson and the customer don't understand each other</u>: When a master leader surveys the sales room (sales pit) or watches his employees on the lot, he'll sometimes notice that a salesperson and customer aren't really communicating and/or getting along. In other words, they do not understand each other, and for whatever reason, the salesperson doesn't even realize that he's not connecting. This is when the leader should think up a good reason to introduce himself into the sales presentation. Again, the leader knows all too well how valuable customers are, and he doesn't want even one of them to get away, much less get away feeling confused, upset, or disrespected. Any communication problem between a salesperson and a customer is a green light for the master leader to step in.

    He can possibly salvage an unlikely sale while giving the salesperson some wise instruction. If the salesperson just steps aside and pays attention, then he can learn some special selling or closing points from the leader and hopefully realize where he got offtrack with his customer.

5. <u>When the master leader wants to make a point</u>: One of the main duties a master leader has (when he has time) is to enthusiastically teach and train his salespeople in the great art

of selling. The sales training exercise is an ongoing affair that never ends. If, during his daily rounds, a master leader sees any of his salespeople making basic sales presentation mistakes while attending customers, miss-steps that could very easily lose his company a sale, then the leader will, if the situation is favorable, step in and take over. The leader will not try to embarrass a salesperson in front of his customer. Only after the customer has left the office will the leader give constructive criticism. When this kind of stepping in action is taken by the leader, the salesperson should stay with the customer (unless asked to leave by the leader) and try to learn a few things. The salesperson, needless to say, should never ask the leader if he's done something wrong or say, "What's wrong?" within earshot of the customer. This only makes the salesperson sound like an amateur and makes the company look like a sales training school.

6. <u>When to wield authority</u>: There are times in the sales business when a salesperson will have a customer who won't do anything with anyone except the boss. A professional salesperson knows that the "let me talk to your supervisor" line is a customer's way of trying to intimidate and get (or so the customer believes) more attention or a better deal. This type of hardball-playing customer can cause problems for salespeople who are rookies or who take his attitude personally. In circumstances like this, the leader should step in and utilize all of his wisdom and closing skills to T.O. and sell this wily customer. The battle-wise veteran leader knows this customer has no real problem with the salesperson other than the fact he thinks he was only dealing with a regular everyday salesman. This legend in his own mind customer believes only the top man can deal with a client of his caliber. It is therefore essential the master leader steps into the situation with an air of complete self-confidence. The leader must be more than a match for the confrontational demeanor of this customer. Even if it's not his style, this is the time for the leader to swagger, dominate the conversation, and turn on his laser-intense eye contact. The

leader's authoritative power is what the customer is expecting, and that's what the leader should deliver. Nine out of ten times, the demanding customer will turn into a harmless little lamb when confronted with a leader who is a master of control and intimidation.

Should the leader mistakenly approach this type of customer with a soft passivity and quiet resolve to be of service, then both the salesperson and the company come away losers. Nice salespeople do close sales, but when the customer is hard-nosed and/or arrogant, the nice salesperson will in most cases finish last.

....

"Financial concerns will always be the principle reason why a customer won't purchase."

MARIE JAQUES, MIAMI, FL

....

7. <u>When the master leader needs sales</u>: No matter the talent and drive a leader has, there will be times when their sales force finds itself in a slump. In these cases the true leader starts working directly with the customers, even if some of his salespeople feel as though he's intruded upon their domain. Somebody in the company has got to get the job of selling done, and at down-and-out moments like these, the master leader will step up to the plate and personally take over. He will, with the enthusiasm of a rookie, leap into the trenches and lead the charge. When the leader starts moving around the sales area, going from customer to customer, interjecting his power and positive input, his salespeople immediately get energized, and in only a few hours, sales production starts turning around for the better. Actions will always speak louder than a pep talk from the sidelines.

    Reader, the master leader is the definite commander of his sales team, and when the team is tiring or starting to sputter, the leader will step in and lead by example.

8.   <u>When a T.O. needs a T.O.</u>: Situations arise when a salesperson will call in a well-qualified sales manager or assistant manager to T.O. his customer. But, as with a lot of well-made plans, things don't go as expected. Often the same problem that prompted the salesperson to call for help is a dilemma for the sales manager. In fact, the sales manager may well need assistance on a difficult question or in dealing with a tough personality. In times like this, the sales manager calls in the master leader to save the whole sales process. When this situation occurs, the sales manager should introduce the leader to the customer, explaining the customer's problem and/or question so everyone at the closing table understands and is on the same page. The sales manager should then excuse himself from the group and leave the customer, the original salesperson, and the master leader alone.

Note: Never should the sales manager, the original salesperson, and leader try to sell the customer simultaneously. There should be only one person who takes control and talks to the customer. If the customer feels like he is being ganged up on or overwhelmed with too much information, then he will walk away without buying anything.

3. When Is the Incorrect Time for the Master Leader To T.O.?

Just as vital as knowing when to take over a customer, it is equally important to know when not to. The wrong timing, the wrong tone of voice, the wrong attitude, or the wrong strategy on the master leader's part could kill a sale faster than someone throwing ice water in the customer's face. Every leader who runs a winning sales team must instinctively know when to stay clear and out of a salesperson-customer relationship. It might appear that negotiations are breaking down (between the salesperson and customer) or there is some sort of disconnect at the closing table, but the wise leader knows to stay away until he is actually called upon and invited into the sales process and and/or discussion. If need be, the salesperson, leader, or sales manager should develop secret signals that say "I need help" or "stay away" to prevent an unnecessary T.O. that could prove to be counterproductive.

"Remember, never walk, talk, or squawk past the 'close'."

MITCH LAMBERT, ANNAPOLIS, MD

---

1. <u>When the salesperson and customer enjoy a good rapport</u>: The master leader never interferes with a salesperson who has established a good relationship with his customer. The leader knows that his salespeople are constantly developing a feeling of trust with their customers during their sales presentations through common bonds.

   Any leader who foolishly intervenes without being invited by a salesperson could create an enemy (the salesperson) and possibly disrupt any positive thoughts the customer might have. The leader can tell the difference between an undeveloped sales closing exercise and a salesperson-customer relationship that has derailed and needs saving.

2. <u>When the customer is silent</u>: When a salesperson has his or her customer in the final closing stages of his sales presentation, the customer, more than likely, will spend some private time silently contemplating whether or not to purchase the product. This very, very important contemplation period or silent review of product notes and product prices might only take a few minutes or a few hours, but, in truth, it feels like an eternity to a salesperson, sales manager, or leader. At this breath-holding time when the customer is in his solemn decision moment, the leader or anyone else should not, for heaven's sake, interfere. When the customer is quiet, the leader doesn't touch. He will keep still and let the salesperson complete the sales transaction in his own good time. No news is not necessarily bad news, and an attempted T.O. during these sensitive seconds

or minutes is likely to backfire. Don't forget, the salesperson has worked for quite a while to get his customer in a positive buying mood. All it takes to break this fragile feeling is one wrong word or an inappropriate move on the part of a leader with good intentions. A master leader knows the difference between nipping a "no" in the bud and annoying a customer who is quietly mulling things over.

3. <u>When the salesperson mis-leads his customer</u>: The master leader has two unwritten responsibilities to the company he either owns or works for. He has to present his company in a very positive light and protect his company's reputation. With this professional code in mind, the leader forbids any of his employees or salespeople to misrepresent his company or its products, or lie to any of his company's customers. Now, if a leader finds one of his employees intentionally being deceitful to a customer, an immediate firing is appropriate. Furthermore, if any employee lies to a customer and a company sales manager or assistant supports the lie, then all parties involved should be fired. An honorable leader will not T.O. for a dishonest salesperson, will not cover up for one, and will not, under any circumstance, tolerate one. The leader, in his wisdom, knows that the customer, his company, and his self-respect are too important to be poisoned by lies, deceit, and mistrust.

....

"To destroy your enemy, ask your enemy for a favor."

THOMAS RAMIREZ, WINSTON-SALEM, NC

....

4. <u>When the salesperson has made an enemy</u>: When a salesperson has inadvertently upset his customer and made him angry, the master leader should fight the temptation to play policeman and, in most cases, just stay away. One must give the customer time, and room, to cool off, even if the leader is convinced his salesperson was at fault.

The leader, if he's not careful, could easily add fuel to the fire if he tries to step in and resolve things while the customer is out of sorts. Salespeople are professionals and if they can't calm down their own customer, then it would be even more difficult for a perfect stranger (the leader) to try to do so. In a problem situation like this, or when the disgruntled customer sits back down at the closing table rather than leaving the sales office, the leader should signal for the salesperson to leave the room. Then outside, beyond the angry customer's "space," the leader should brief the salesperson and coach him on some quick crisis management.

Note: Angry customers mostly want to vent and will initially strike at anyone who will try to help or listen. Once the upset customer relaxes for a few minutes on his own, he can be approached and gently reasoned with. If the leader honestly feels his personality will be beneficial, then by all means he should get involved. Remember, sales is a people game, and in that game there are many unknowns. The best thing a salesperson can do is be non-combative, pleasant, and a little humble; realize the old saying "humility has no enemies" is very true.

"If a customer doesn't feel special and appreciated,
he won't hear one word the salesperson says."

Mort Cohen, Atlantic City, NJ

4. Special Note Regarding Customers

The master leader knows better than anyone that customers are only real people. They are not monsters who can destroy or humiliate a person in two minutes or less, and they are not all do-gooders who are incapable of doing any wrong. Customers are folks with varying interests, fears, and feelings. They want only two fundamental things in life from their fellow man: to be loved and respected. The true leader gives out daily abundance of these two wants to everyone he meets. When he dispenses these precious needs, the world around him improves and his position in life will never be questioned or seriously challenged.

The leader treats every customer he takes over as though they were the only client he was going to have all year long. With this kind of intense caring showered on a grateful customer, the leader's closing percentages will go through the roof. The master leader's secret for closing customers is simple. He takes the time to understand each customer's needs and/or problems, he shows empathy, he patiently probes their doubts and questions, and then he tells the customer the truth about owning and financing his product. When all of these steps are taken in a respectful and enthusiastic sales presentation, the leader will sell nearly everyone he talks to. Even customers who appear rude, moody, or greedy can't resist the leader's enchanting and honest personality.

Note: Love and respect are far from the whole story here. The master leader also uses an array of learned sales techniques, multiple psychological methods, and various closing maneuvers to guide his customer to a positive "viewing place," where the advantages of owning his product are more clearly seen. This viewing place is one that illustrates the products value in real life without objections or preconceived notions from the client, and allows the leader the opportunity to fully engage the client towards a sale.

Reader, leaders know for a fact that most customers don't really mind a hard or even aggressive sale just as long as they feel they are being told the truth and being treated fairly.

....

"Well done is better than well said"

BEN FRANKLIN

....

6.

The Master Leader "Takes Over" and "Closes"

CHAPTER 6

(THE DELICATE ART OF THE T.O.)

Every company in the world needs a strong and sales-oriented master leader to ensure lasting sales success. The leader is the one personal ally employees and salespeople depend on to keep all divisions and departments of the company running smoothly and profitably. The leader, knowing his or her personality, will, when necessary, help his salespeople sell. This is when the leader shows his sales expertise and takes over for his sales force. This delicate

T.O. operation is the subject of the following pages. The practice of closing and taking over a customer is not to be taken lightly. Closing a customer on a product is a very serious business; it involves real money, real feelings, and a fair balance of enthusiasm, faith, trust, and showmanship.

> *"If a leader can't sell a customer with all he has at his disposal, then he needs to get out of the business."*
>
> ALLEN ROSS, CHICAGO, IL

1. SETTING THE STAGE FOR A T.O. OPERATION

Before the take over or turn over procedure is discussed, the stage has to be set so you, the reader, can envision the overall environment and atmosphere in which a T.O. operation takes place.

Note: Company sales divisions all differ. Some use only phone rooms or have salespeople working certain areas in states or territories. Some companies might use individual sales offices or closing rooms. For our topic on the T.O., we'll use a single sales office with one central sales area, as in an automobile dealership. This sales area (closing room) could be large enough to hold anywhere from fifty to one hundred salespeople and their customers. In this kind of energy-charged environment, we will look at the master leader and see how he professionally implements the T.O. for his sales team.

So here we go. In the exciting setting of a large sales closing room, the master leader (when he has the time) will stand back, usually in a corner, and constantly watch all of the activity that is taking place on the sales floor. The leader waits here with restless patience for one of his salespeople or sales managers to come up to him and ask for help in selling a customer. Or, in some cases, the leader waits for a salesperson to raise his hand, indicating that he needs help immediately.

Reader, the following illustrations and guidelines will take you, step by serious step, through an entire take over operation so you can experience and learn certain T.O. methods without any difficulty.

Note: The instructions here, like most human endeavors, are not carved in stone. Anything can happen during a T.O. situation, and the master leader (because of his experience) will be able to adjust to any unexpected circumstance. When faced with crises, the wise leader will never get thrown off guard or lose his composure. Here is a little side note of interest. Sometimes when the leader is called to a closing table by one of his salespeople, the customer will, instead of digging in for battle, simply say when they see the leader, "OK. I'll purchase the product." When this happens, and it does happen, the leader or salesperson should stop talking about the product, congratulate the customer on his decision, and write up the order. There will always be surprising times when the leader has to throw the sales rule book out the window and just fly by the seat of his pants. If a leader has to strictly live by some instruction book, then he needs to get another job.

> *"When I 'T.O.' customers, I present a gentle, attentive, and disciplined demeanor."*
>
> BETTY MAHON, LONG ISLAND, NY

2. THE T.O. DRAMA

The master leader understands that there are three major acts in the T.O. drama:

Act I—The Approach

When a salesperson is sitting with his customer at the closing table and he has, for whatever reason, been unable to get his customer to make a buying decision, there are several unobtrusive ways to call in the leader for help or assistance:

1. Matter-of-factly tell his customer that he should get further clarification on the product and that it would be helpful if the leader could explain things from a different perspective,

suggesting that the added advice and/or information would be to the customer's benefit.

2. Wait for a complex question, allowing the salesperson to enthusiastically announce that he'll ask his leader to come in and respond.

3. Tell his customer that he doesn't have the authority to act on the customer's request. His (the customer's) inquiry deserves to be considered, so it's time to talk to the master leader.

Any and all of these simple excuses will work for the salesperson, but he has got to keep control of his customer and make sure he doesn't walk away when he (the salesperson) is out locating the leader.

A professional salesperson will enact the necessary tact and speed to bring the leader into the scene. This is when the leader makes his initial approach. Cheerful, serious, and confident, the leader walks up to the closing table and joins in the negotiations.

Act II—The Close

Once everyone is comfortably seated and all introductions have been made, the leader gets the pertinent information from the salesperson relating to the customer's problem and/or questions. The leader plans his primary game based on the circumstances and his assessment of the customer, implementing whichever T.O. techniques or maneuvers necessary. Here the master leader calls on his years of acquired knowledge to close (seal) the deal and have the customer sign the contract.

Act III—The Exit

Once the customer has signed the work sheet or contract, the master leader graciously excuses himself and exits the scene. The deal is done; the leader leaves the salesperson with his customer to wrap up any details.

Now, these are the major basic steps that have to be taken, in exact order, for the leader to productively T.O. But, within each step, there are important substeps that also have to be well executed for a professional T.O. to really work.

These essential additional steps are explained in the following take over notes.

....

"If a customer likes you, they will listen to you, they will believe you, and if they believe you, then they will buy."

SUSAN COFFMAN, ORLANDO, FL

....

3. IMPORTANT SALES AND PSYCHOLOGICAL NOTES TO KEEP IN MIND WHEN TAKING OVER

Watch the Sales Area—Again, the master leader is the overall boss of the company's sales office, and it is his responsibility to know everything possible that is going on all around him. The leader has to be acutely aware of all of his salespeople's performance in the sales area. When a sales room closing pit is really buzzing with high energy (the salespeople and customers talking, squawking, and discussing), there must be someone in complete control. It doesn't matter if it's a boiler room full of people on the phone or a car lot with customers and salespeople chasing each other. One powerful individual who knows and sees all the parts of the puzzle and how they are placed together to make the whole day, week, month, and year progressive and successful. The master leader is the orchestra leader with all of his salespeople playing different instruments. His job is making sure every individual plays their part to the best of their ability but in harmony with everyone else.

1. <u>Be the problem solver:</u> The master leader who is called in to T.O. a salesperson's customer is being looked up to as the problem solver. He is seen as the one person who can help sell a customer and get him down on paper (initial signing of a contract) The customer and the salesperson are expecting many things out of the leader in a T.O. situation. The customer first sees the leader as the only person with enough authority and knowledge to make him feel confident and secure in

purchasing the product. Second, the customer expects the leader to stand with him if he has any product problems down the road. Third, the customer wants to feel that he can send his friends to the leader knowing they will be received with a warm welcome and treated with respect.

Note: If any leader first addresses a customer with an attitude of weakness or an inflection of self-doubt, there will be no sale. The leader knows that a customer will size him up and have a private impression of him in only five to seven seconds.

2. <u>Set the nervous customer at ease:</u> The master leader realizes when he is called to T.O. the customer will most likely be edgy, scared, or nervously reserved. This is why it is so very important for the leader to radiate a quiet authority that won't challenge or intimidate a sensitive customer. The leader purposely gives the customer some time to mentally adjust to him and his added presence at the closing table. The customer has got to have a feeling of calm or he will think the T.O. leader is there to bully, push, and pressure.

   If a leader just walks up to a nervous customer and immediately starts hammering away using hardball closes (without so much as a sincere "Hello"), then it's guaranteed the customer will jump up from the closing table and run out the sales office door. And, in truth, who can blame him?

"All customers have secrets they want to disclose to someone they trust."

DOYLE THOMPSON, MOBILE, AL

---

3. <u>Listen to the customer:</u> When a master leader goes in to take over for a salesperson, he had better (after the introductions are made) be quiet and listen to the customer describe his difficulties with the product being sold. It's crucial the leader hears the whole story and not assume what the customer is about to say or cut him off in midsentence. Even if the leader has heard

the same customer comments a thousand times before, the leader will appear genuinely interested and respectful. Reader, the leader was called to the closing table to solve a problem, not to impatiently preempt one. The T.O. situation is not always the last minute before the buzzer sounds; it is, in many cases, a time to finesse points rather than burst in for a slam dunk. The leader completely understands that customers are not stupid, and they can see in the leader's eyes whether he really cares or whether he only sees checks and commissions. A person's eyes tell all. Any so-called leader who thinks that he and his selfish motives can hide behind a smooth voice, charming words, and a firm handshake is only fooling himself. The true leader knows that sincere respect and concern will (in a few minutes) radiate from his eyes and, of course as most believe, the eyes are the windows of the soul.

4. <u>Be authoritative but humble:</u> All master leaders should act like an important director when they get to a closing table to T.O., but they also should project a subtle air of being decent and humble. This fine balance in the art of personality behavior has been developed over the years by the master leader via everyday trials and errors. The leader is a professional performer who delivers his lines upon the pillars of truth. A leader cannot go into a T.O. concern with an outlook that radiates a snobbish and egotistical "I know it all" disposition. Most, if not all, customers will not put up with some wise guy leader who is trying to show off his closing abilities or sales techniques for the whole sales office to see. If in this instance a customer doesn't immediately walk out the door, then he might play the game for a half hour or so and then refuse to sign the contract. On the other hand, even customers who despise the carnival barker's hard sell expect the T.O. man (the leader) to be strong and assertive. Their expectations are linked to the leader's title and their personal case. The master leader will pleasantly surprise the customer by conforming to their presumed vision of him but also displaying a genuine kindness that cannot be contested or ignored.

5. <u>Tell a background story:</u> When the master leader first meets a customer in his high-powered role of being a T.O. for one of his salespeople, he should gently break the ice and tension with a warm-up story somewhat related to the product. The leader should tell the customer some personal anecdote or introduce some non-threatening conversation designed to relax the customer. For example: "Mr. Customer, I noticed your school ring. I've got an embarrassing story to tell you about my own school ring…" This background warm-up story could be something about the leader's family, past experiences, or job, anything intimate and/or personal. This easy and pleasant warm-up story must be a sincere gesture of friendliness that can't be interpreted as a phony ploy or distraction. The customer has to have a good feeling towards the leader, or there won't be a sale. All people prefer to do business with a trusted friend, and the easiest way to make a friend out of a stranger is to share personal information that creates an immediate familiarity and bond.

....

"Common bonds unite, but a passion for that common bond embraces."

RICARDO ARAGON, SAN FRANCISCO, CA

....

6. <u>Kick the salesperson if needed:</u> When a salesperson asks his master leader to sit down at the closing table with his customer for a T.O., the spotlight and microphone switches from the salesperson to the leader. From the very moment the leader is introduced to the customer, the salesperson should sit perfectly still (not chewing gum) and pay *respectful* attention to what is being said.

The obedient salesperson (unless asked to leave the table) should politely confirm his leader's statements with soft and gently affirmative nods of the head and speak only (and we mean *only*) when spoken to.

Note: If the salesperson is jeopardizing hundreds of thousands of dollars because he can't keep his mouth shut or wants to get his two cents' worth in, then the leader should either kick the salesperson's leg under the table or shoot him a shut-your-trap look. When the leader is talking to the customer, the salesperson must not throw the leader's timing or train of thought off by interrupting or making unnecessary physical movements. The salesperson should only continue to be involved if he and the leader have a running dialogue planned out in advance.

7. Keep everyone involved: When the master leader sits down at the closing table with the salesperson and several other people (or family members) who make up the customer's party, he (the leader) had better have enough sense to keep everyone present involved in the overall conversation. The leader never leaves anyone out in left field. Whether it's the spouse or the second cousin of the principle client, the leader knows invariably that either the one person who is ignored will feel somewhat slighted or hostile and could turn into the opposition element that kills the sale or the person left out is the one with all the money and final purchasing say-so. The leader also knows that winning over a spouse or child could be enough extra leverage to turn a reluctant customer into a buyer. The leader understands that everyone sitting around the closing table helps make the buying decision even if they don't have speaking parts in the drama.

"Emotions sell. Logic, materialistic thoughts, charts, graphs, and calculations come in a distant second."

PATRICIA YORK, DALLAS, TX

8. Divorce the extra couple: When the master leader is called to a closing table by a salesperson and the customer has his friends with him (as opposed to members of his immediate family), the leader, if he feels it's necessary to get a sale, should politely ask the customer's friends (the tagalongs) to excuse

themselves so he and the customer can discuss personal financial matters. The leader, not wanting to hurt anyone's feelings and not wanting to upset anyone, should graciously invite the extra guests to the company's lobby area for coffee. The leader will be courteous but firm in his request. He knows from years of experience that tagalongs can and, in most cases, will cause trouble. Generally speaking, customers won't buy if their friends oppose the purchase. The leader's line about respecting private financial information is not just a line. Many customers feel very uncomfortable discussing their money matters in front of friends.

9. <u>Don't jump around:</u> The master leader will keep an eye on the whole closing room floor and will meet and greet customers at his leisure. He will casually walk between the closing tables to get a feel of the room, but once he has been asked to T.O., he will concentrate on that one case alone.

    He will take his place at the closing table he's been invited to and will stay there until he sells. He will not jump around from closing table to closing table, juggling customers as though they were bowling pins. Customers want to feel unique and important, and they don't want to see the distinguished leader who has taken part of his valuable time to personally come over and see them, rushing off every few minutes like a hyper, uncontrolled, crazy person. Customers are very alert and always watching what goes on around them. In fact, customers are a lot more observant, intelligent, and sensitive than many salespeople and sales managers realize. The T.O. situation only heightens this sensitivity. If customers are treated like numbers and percentages and not special individual humans, then any sales quota the leader was wanting or needing will simply vanish into thin air.

10. <u>Know the salesperson's habits:</u> The professional leader should generally know the selling habits and modes of operation of each of his salespeople. In other words, the leader has to know each personality working on his sales team. Leaders can easily learn these through observation over a period of four weeks or

twenty customers, whichever comes first. The leader realizes for any T.O. to be successful that coordinating facts along with an agreeable transition from the salesperson to him are vital. That's why the leader will ask several questions to find a base line, and even mimic the salespersons stance or voice inflection to ensure a smooth transfer. Individual selling and closing styles should not be so jarringly different that a customer feels confused.

"Customers always have the freedom to go to any company where they feel comfortable."

TERRI LOWELL, SALT LAKE CITY, UT

11. Let your face be known: Whenever possible, the master leader makes it a point to say "Hello" to every single customer who comes into his sales office. This planned but easy and soft greeting actually preconditions every customer, allowing them to get used to the leader's face. This way, should the leader be called in to T.O. a customer, he won't be some threatening stranger who arrives out of nowhere. He's the friendly person the customer briefly met earlier. Now, the leader doesn't have to stand (like a doorman) at the front door of his sales office to accomplish this preconditioning ritual, he can politely say "Hello" at any appropriate moment after the customer and salesperson are paired off.

    Note: This is an old but good psychological tip to remember when greeting customers—the master leader should use the word "Today" at every opportunity. For example, "How are you today, Mr. Customer?" "Isn't today beautiful?" or "Good to see you today." The customer keeps that word (today) floating around in his subconscious, and in a few minutes the customer (out of his own thinking) realizes that all the sales operations he is going to be exposed to are designed to do business *today*, not tomorrow or down the road.

12. Be yourself: Any T.O. situation can be a nerve-racking, unsettling, and awkward affair.

Again, a leader who over-performs and tries to put on some elaborate show hoping to impress his sales force will only make things a lot worse. Nothing irritates a customer more than a leader who initially impresses one as a phony or a silver-tongued devil trying to break the ice by telling a joke he can't deliver properly. No matter what, the master leader has to be himself or herself, never doubting or trying to cover up his own unique personality. If the salesperson's customer needs a little time to get used to the leader, then the leader should ask some very general and friendly questions rather than attempting to entertain and/or be majestic. Whenever a so-called leader puts on a mask, it soon starts to peel off and all the truth begins to show.

13. <u>Train sales managers and assistants to T.O.:</u> The master leader has a professional obligation to educate and train his subordinates in the fine art of the T.O. He is responsible for teaching his salespeople everything he knows so they in turn can help and instruct others. The leader understands that in order to be successful, he has to surround himself with successful people.

··

"If a director looses control of his emotions, the damage done is irreparable."

DON NASCH, NEW YORK, NY

··

14. <u>Don't lose composure:</u> Whether the negotiating action at the closing table is good, bad, or ugly, the master leader should not get overly emotional and lose his composure. The leader has to keep his dignity and leadership role intact. If the leader, because of some irrational, unforeseen circumstance, becomes provoked, exasperated, or downright angry, then everyone and everything around him will instantly fall to pieces. The leader is the captain of the ship, and everyone turns to him when a severe storm kicks up. If the leader loses his temper and throws a fit for all to see, then he is in essence giving the rest of his employees the right to do the same. Plus, if the leader

acts unprofessional, even for a minute, it is very likely everyone's respect for him will plummet. Working the T.O. pressure table is bound to result in some nerve-fraying experiences and occasional insensitive remarks, but the leader has to stay in polite control. If, for whatever reason, the customer throws out insults and intentionally provokes, then the leader should simply walk away and stay away. It's a whole lot smarter to lose one sale than to lose a whole closing room full of sales.

4. Special Note About Master Leaders

Master leaders know their company and their employees better than anyone, and they should because their whole existence depends on that knowledge. If, as stated before, the leader has to wash dishes, T.O., make reservations for clients, give meetings, or write reports, then he will.

He leads by example, and he knows customers are clever, employees sometimes try to hide, salespeople complain, and office staff want more money. The leader is not senseless or shallow, he understands, and he does all in his power to make his people feel important and needed. The leader stresses the principles of attitude and enthusiasm, and tells their employees that anyone talking without a positive outlook is only a person making noise. The power of enthusiasm is what sells, not logic.. All leaders know that positive energy produces positive results just like the saying, "If you do what's right, then things will be all right." The master leader is a person who is not afraid; he will stand his ground and represent his company and employees until the very end of his duties. He knows in his heart a person's words mean nothing if spoken without conviction. Every day the leader teaches his people psychological survival skills needed in today's highly complex international business market. The master leader is a champion's champion and, in his wisdom, strives to make those around him the same, if not better.

"A sales presentation without conviction makes you look like a convict"

JWW & JWP

7.

Keeping the Office On Track

CHAPTER 7

THE MASTER LEADER KEEPS THE SALES OPERATION ON TRACK

Now reader, let's fast-forward; after the sales office's first year of business, the sales force under the master leader's direction has done its job. The sales volume and closing percentages posted are phenomenal. But, as with any company in the world, there will always be a small percentage of customers who want to cancel their sales contracts. It's just part of the selling profession. This is when the master leader can once again come to his sales employees' rescues and retain a fickle customer and/or save a deal.

"The leader always has been, and always will be, the moral compass of his company."

KENNETH STOLTZ, BEVERLY HILLS, CA

1. FIVE BASIC REASONS CUSTOMERS CANCEL

1. <u>Simple buyer's remorse:</u> Buyer's remorse is when the customer gets cold feet about a purchase. He (for a hundred reasons) starts to have second and third thoughts on every little thing about the product right after he signs the sales contracts. The true reason most customers have buyer's remorse isn't the product, or for that matter, the salesperson—it's themselves.

   The customer who usually gets scared and wants to cancel his sales contract lacks confidence in himself and his ability to live up to the terms of the contract. This kind of customer probably has a history of turning his back on commitments or honoring a firm pledge. Buyer's remorse is a sad phenomenon that happens to weaker customers. They are the people, in general, who get caught up in the salesperson's powerful and enthusiastic sales presentation and, in an uncharacteristic spark of energy, decide to purchase the product on the spot. Then, after the salesperson has left and they don't have a cheerleader to keep them enthused, they come out from under the ether, look at themselves, and say, "What happened?" This is when they want to cancel.

   Since the customer with buyer's remorse doubts and questions his own actions, the master leader (when he talks to this customer) must build the customer's confidence in himself and the product. The leader has to convince the doubting

Thomas that he has made a sound and intelligent purchase. This nervous customer is just the candidate for the leader to explain that a deal is a deal and having second thoughts doesn't automatically erase a legal and binding contract. The leader can use friendly persuasion, or he can resort to the powerful weapon of shame to rein this wishy-washy customer in.

Note: A lot of salespeople don't realize this, but a customer needs (in his own mind) permission to purchase a product. Now, this consent, where he realizes it will be fine to buy, might come from a family member, friends, or from the customer himself. Many customers have to know that they won't be laughed at or ridiculed for their decision.

When a customer feels good knowing everyone he respects will approve his purchase, then the chances of him changing his mind are minimized.

....

"Sympathy and understanding always get better results than threats and condemnation."

HELEN FISHER, CINCINNATI, OH

....

2. <u>Found a better deal:</u> Another straightforward reason for a customer's cancellation involves the customer finding a better price at another company or dealership. In a case like this, there is no blame to be felt by anyone. The curious customer, after inking a deal, just happens upon the same product for a more reasonable price with maybe a better guarantee or more extras. This of course is all the excuse the customer thinks he needs to justify an immediate cancellation of his signed contract. Saving money at another company is all too often worth more to a customer than keeping one's word. Lest we think that today's business world is populated with scheming customers victimizing innocent salespeople, it was probably the competing salesman with the better deal who showed the customer just how to cancel out on his first contract.

For the master leader to save this kind of customer, he could cut his profit margin by matching the other company's price or by adding extra incentives, making the product more desirable to the customer. If, after some friendly negotiating, the customer still wants out of the contract, the leader must weigh the economic options.

Would the leader's company lose more from the loss of one sale than it would cost to take legal action? If taking the customer to court is economically feasible, then it's time for the leader to remind the customer that a judgment might be necessary. Most likely, the customer will see that abusing his contractual agreement will end up costing him much more than it might save him.

3. <u>Lack of funds:</u> It's not uncommon at all for the customer to get home after purchasing a product, appraise his expenses, and realize that he simply can't afford the product. This type of customer most typically (like a lot of customers) got caught up in the salesperson's enthusiasm and signed the sales contract at a moment when his desire for the product exceeded his financial capabilities.

   The master leader must remember this kind of customer genuinely wanted to purchase the product and the only real obstacle is purely monetary. In a case like this, the leader should have a heart-to-heart talk with the customer and explain to him that he was once in the very same financial position. The leader should make the customer feel that his satisfaction in this situation is more desirable than his money and generously try to help the customer work out a budget plan that will comfortably allow the customer to keep the product and not cancel the sale. The creative leader could offer the customer better terms for referring new customers to his sales office or could offer advice on loans, etc. The customer might need a reminder that canceling out on a legal sales contract is bad for one's credit rating. If all fails and the customer really can't afford the product, then the leader should graciously let the customer off the hook and cordially invite him back when his finances are in better order.

"If you confuse the customer, you lose the customer. It's that simple."

CAROL PATTERSON, DES MOINES, IA

4. <u>Lack of understanding:</u> Sometimes a customer seems to understand the general meaning of the sales document he has signed, but in reality he doesn't fully grasp the finer details. The customer gets home and slowly goes over the contract without the distractions of the salesperson and closing room and, lo and behold, he discovers that the contract doesn't exactly state what he expected it to. The customer panics and alerts the sales office that he is going to cancel.

   The master leader knows that reviewing the sales contract at the closing table is the responsibility of the salesperson and the sales manager. He (the leader) is also aware that too many salespeople hate to go over contracts in detail. Salespeople do not have the temperament of lawyers, so one can't really condemn them for kind of skimming over the contract and only pointing out and stressing the important parts. In fact, most salespeople hope for the customer to be happy and to put the signed sales contract away in some desk and forget about it.

   Note: "Buyer Beware" is the customer's credo, but the salesperson who glosses over contracts because of laziness or deceit is only courting customer cancellations or worse. In a situation where the customer didn't comprehend the entire sales contract or some crucial detail, it is up to the master leader or his associates to re-educate and resell the product to the customer with complete clarity and understanding. Don't forget, the customer did initially want the product, so he warrants the extra time and effort to smooth over any and all rough spots. Attempts to intimidate this kind of customer will only backfire. He'll then be convinced that the leader's company was out to get him with all the confusing fine print.

5. <u>The customer feels cheated:</u> Reader, there will always be customers (because of human nature) who cancel their sales contract because they honestly believe they were lied to or

cheated in some way. These kinds of customers might have seen a negative new bulletin or read about some recall regarding the product they just purchased. Maybe they feel that a salesperson flatly misrepresented the product, or they believe they paid too much for the product. When the master leader is faced with a customer who feels in his heart that he was, in one way or another, hoodwinked, the best thing the leader can do, besides try and re-sell the customer, is twofold: prove he was not deceived or taken advantage of and either give the customer his money back or give him a new product with some extras.

The leader must always avoid a scandal for his company, and if this customer becomes explosive, threatening to call in lawyers or the attorney general, the leader's wisdom will always prevail by calming the customer, satisfying the customer, and for heaven's sake, letting the customer walk away.

"The leader doesn't let pain, excuses, tension, or fright outline their goals in life."

DAWN VARGAS, OLYMPIA, WA

2. THE MASTER LEADER'S REACTION TO CANCELLATIONS

When a master leader first finds out that a customer wants to cancel his sales contract, he's naturally going to be upset. The leader, as we know, has a position where he has to be seen as unshakable, a person who doesn't fall apart when things go badly. The leader understands when a customer wants out of a deal it's most likely (as stated before) just a case of cold feet. The first step for the leader is to call the customer's salesperson into his office to discover any clues why the customer is having second thoughts. If the salesperson can't come up with any motive, then the second step is to invite the customer back into the sales office so the leader can have a home court advantage for a face-to-face meeting. The leader can take control or let the original salesperson talk to the customer; it all depends on what kind of rapport the salesperson had with the client.

The leader realizes time is of the essence when a customer wants to cancel, but good judgment must also be applied; some customers need to be revisited, resold, and appealed to immediately, while others need a couple of days to let their nerves settle. Now, before the leader talks to the problem customer, he has to mentally erase any traces of disappointment or frustration and adopt an air of sincere concern and care. After the problem customer is back in the leader's office, the leader should disarm the customer with a "good loser" attitude, letting the customer think he has won and that he can easily get out of the purchase. In fact, the customer might have shown up at the leader's office ready to do battle, but he (the customer) does not realize being all alone with the leader will make it a lot tougher to cancel. The leader should not jump right into the middle of the problem, but first extend a warm welcome that usually melts away any antagonism. And, as always, he must listen to the customer about his concerns. The leader knows that in many cases a problem customer will honor the sales contract if someone of importance in the company just takes the time to patiently "hold hands" and understand the customer's dilemma. Remember, anger or self-righteousness will only reinforce the problem customer's resolve to fight. The truth is, in any congenial atmosphere the leader creates, it's very hard for the problem customer to remain hostile and uncooperative. In this calm environment, the leader takes his time, agrees and disagrees with the customer, makes his positive points about the product, reinforces the customer's self-confidence, and saves the sale.

"Most customers who want to nullify a sales contract feel they are victims."

CARRIE DASHLIN, SCRANTON, PA

3. Important Tips Concerning Customer Who Want to Cancel

1. Remember that buyers can be liars: Problem customers will lie all day long to a master leader, trying their very best to get out of a sales contract. They'll fib about any number of things including: what their salesperson told them; what they did not understand concerning some contract clause; the product not working right or as advertised; what the guarantee states; having to sign the contract under duress of a hard sell. Problem customers will stay up all night scheming elaborate plans and stories to get out of the deal.

2. Handle the shoulder chip: Again, because this is important, no matter how powerful, stubborn, or defensive the problem customer acts when he comes back into the master leader's sales office to cancel his contract, he's still downright scared and intimidated. The customer with a chip on the shoulder knows that the leader's company is unhappy with him, and he honestly doesn't know how he is going to be received. He's in enemy territory, so he has his guard up. That "cancellation chip" can always be smoothly removed by the leader who treats this problem customer with unexpected understanding. The leader, as always, takes gentle control, finds a face-saving solution for the customer, and rescues the sale.

3. Keep control: No matter what happens at this very volatile time, when a resell operation or cancellation hangs in the balance, the master leader must keep all conversations and emotions from getting hateful and/or out of hand. In a single flash of anger, everything could blow up and any hope of saving a deal would be gone forever. The leader must be strong and courageous enough to defuse any indignity with sensitivity and level-headedness. Sometimes, the leader can even confide in a customer with a grievance that he has a legitimate complaint, and the company policy really needs to be amended. The leader should thank the customer for helping

bring up this flaw that will be addressed at the next organizational meeting. The leader will explain to the customer (in soft and sympathetic tones) how he must execute the company's policy in the meantime, despite his own personal regrets. The problem customer, in most cases, will be impressed with this kind of integrity, and the cancellation might be dropped.

4. <u>Don't apologize:</u> When a problem customer is complaining to the master leader about the product, the leader might agree if the product is defective in some way, but should not make the apology sound like a general or standard response for the overall company.

5. <u>Understand that customers want to believe:</u> —When a problem customer is complaining to the master leader about the product, the leader might agree if the product is defective in some way, but the leader should make sure his apology never sounds like a general apology for his overall company.

....

"The practical way to save and resell a problem customer is to reinforce what they like about the product."

BARBARA LAKE, TUCSON, AZ

....

6. <u>Don't solve two customers' problems together:</u> If the master leader has two unrelated problem customers who both want to cancel their contracts at the same time, the leader had better keep these two parties away from each other. If the two different customers come together, this grumbling duo will most likely unite in their complaints and anger, thus feeding off of each other and disrupting the entire sales office.

7. <u>After the save, "shut up":</u> The master leader knows and teaches his salespeople to shut up after a cancellation has been saved. Once the customer is happy again and everything has been ironed out, the salesperson should change subjects and not

mention the product again. If a foolish salesperson or sales manager keeps talking about the product after all problems are solved, then there is a great chance all negotiations will be jeopardized. Most smart salespeople understand "talking got a deal, but more talking can kill a deal."

8. <u>Let the customer cancel:</u> If a leader ever finds himself begging for that save or working too hard with a customer whose problem lies within his psychological makeup, then he must stop! Forget the sale. It's not worth it. The leader's self-respect and sanity are more important. Let the customer cancel, and forget it.

9. <u>Notice who carries the contract:</u> When the master leader sees a customer walking toward his sales office and he knows the customer is coming to cancel, the leader will watch to see which person in the customer's party actually has the contract in hand. In nine out of ten customers, the person who is holding the contract is the person who makes all the decisions and is the person to focus on when trying to re-sell and save.

10. <u>Don't hide:</u> All master leaders are tempted at least once or twice in their professional life to run and hide from an enraged customer who wants to cancel. Of course, this temporary and amateur way out is not the answer. The leader, as we all know, is the captain and will not hide behind a rock, expecting the troops to take all the fire. The leader will stand firm, be brave, show conviction and stand firm even if their knees are shaking a little. Reader, it goes with the territory. If you want to be a master leader, then look, act, and think like one.

....

"A troublemaker doesn't want success; he or she just wants attention."

JAMES WELMON, DENVER, CO

....

4. Special Notes Concerning Problem Employees

If the master leader has an uncontrollable employee or salesperson that just keeps breaking the company's policies, talking negatively, and questioning everything, including authority, then he or she needs to be fired immediately. Period. Leaders understand that after they have terminated a troubled employee they need to take precautions to try to prevent the fired person from stealing away customers, other employees, and/or intentionally and maliciously talking badly about the company and its products. The leader, before taking any legal action, will always consider any and all solutions while wisely remembering the following information:

1. Troubled employees don't like themselves: The master leader understands one very important thing about problem employees. They are mostly troubled simply because they don't like themselves. A lot of disgruntled employees are generally frustrated because they feel they are not as successful or financially sound as they think they should be. By carrying this mental burden, they subconsciously go around with a lot of stored up anger, always looking at the dark side of life, and resenting others who seem more fulfilled. Any problem employee can be helped if he or she wants to face reality and put the blame for his current predicament where it squarely belongs—on himself. But, as human nature goes, most tortured employees can't face the sobering truth and have to point at others for their shortcomings.

   This, in turn, only creates more problems. Leaders know the troubled employee lives in a vicious and maddening circle, always running away from themselves but never escaping. The fact is, how a person treats other people is just a reflection of how he or she feels about themselves.

2. Problem employees will try to steal customers: The master leader must realize, as a cold-hearted fact, that there will always be some problem employees (after they get fired) who

will, out of resentment, try to steal away their old customers from their previous job and take them to their new employer. These kinds of dishonorable ex-employees do exist, and in their minds (for getting terminated) they want to seek some kind of revenge. The leader has to be ever alert and aware of this type of ex-employee. The leader can protect himself by locking away all customer information and by not letting the ex-employee back on his property without permission. The leader has to be vigilant and keen on any unusual activity concerning his customers and his customer-generating problems. Customers mean money, and an angry ex-employee knows this specific all too well.

3. <u>Troubled employees will try to disrupt production:</u> Some problem employees feel if they can't be viewed as super productive or important (with some title or meaningful position), then no one else should be.

   Because of this negative-spiritedness, many troubled employees go out of their way to disrupt progress or make normal, everyday operations difficult for the master leader. For instance, if the leader asks this kind of employee to do something for the office staff or sales team, the problem employee will only do it half-heartedly, without any enthusiasm, and ignore the concept of company spirit. Or, if the leader asks the problem employee to entertain some other employee's client, he will intentionally say nothing to inspire, encourage, or comfort the client. Problem employees of this makeup walk around the company with a frozen frown and jealous emotions flooding their hearts. These sad emotions affect everyone they associate with or talk to.

"People fail because they get tired of trying to succeed. The secret of success is never, never, give up."

DEAN BRISTOL, HICKORY, NC

4. <u>Problem employees borrow money from everyone:</u> The master leader can tell an employee is in trouble when the employee keeps borrowing money from other people in the company and won't come to him (the leader) for advice or assistance. The leader knows that an employee with financial worries is someone who won't focus on their duties as expected. Most employees with money concerns are too embarrassed to discuss them with the leader, fearing they might lose their job.

   No matter the cause of a monetary dilemma, the leader realizes that an employee who goes around asking others for a loan is not good for business. Not only will the borrower be shunned and talked about (petty gossip), but he won't be a strong and independent member of the organization any longer. In the long run, the problem employee will wind up resenting those who avoid them, thus generating a negative atmosphere that doesn't favor him, his colleagues, or his company.

5. <u>Troubled employees will spread rumors:</u> It's nearly impossible for the master leader to prevent nasty little rumors from circulating around the company. Unless the rumor monger is identified and punished, it's very difficult to guard against falsehoods because dirty gossip can swell up from any place at any time. In many cases concerning rumors, the problem employee who is the gossip carrier is, in reality, a person who is just downright jealous of others or the leader himself. This kind of employee, in some instances, thinks that he can do a better job of managing than the leader. So, the problem employee starts spreading fictitious tales about the leader to undermine him and/or make him look bad. Now, this rumor topic might sound too childish to even discuss, but in today's cutthroat business world, rumors and innuendos can, if not quashed, destroy. The leader's only great weapon against harmful talk and nonsense is to be professional, above board, and a champion of integrity.

Again, the leader must, at all times, conduct himself in such a respectable way that any rumors about his performance or his company's reputation prove to be exactly what they sound like—rumors. Problem employees come and go, but a true leader demonstrating class will always be around to usher in greatness, progress, and prosperity.

"Any person who intentionally hurts others
is only declaring war on themselves."

LELAND WILLIS, BILOXI, MS

6. <u>Problem employees will go behind the master leader's back:</u> Any troubled employee who dislikes his leader (for whatever reason) will not only try to make petty problems for them, but also go to the company's owner (if that's the case) and tell little lies or exaggerate some office incident—anything to make the master leader look incompetent. Honestly, no one needs this type of weasel around. In addition to hurting the leader to some degree, he's destroying himself by succumbing to dirty tactics that won't work anyway. The leader can only protect himself from this type of slanderous individual by consistently being the true professional. The leader must fight the urge to retaliate because in the final bout, truth always defeats inaccuracy and fabrication.

7. <u>Troubled employees want help:</u> The master leader understands that no employee is so bad or corrupt that given a little time and attention, their good side starts to peek through all the roughness and sharp edges.

    Problem employees can turn it all around if they have someone who really believes in them and keeps encouraging them. The leader knows that a few kind words or even a sincere handshake can change people's lives. Small things count, and every positive nod of the head, wink, or smile could be just enough to make the problem employee think, "If others like me, then why shouldn't I like myself?" Boom! The whole world changes.

"In the course of things, if a leader can't admit his mistakes, then he shouldn't expect others to."

TRACY RICHARDS, SEATTLE, WA

8.

The Master Leader's Guide for Success

CHAPTER 8

THE MASTER LEADER'S
GUIDE FOR SUCCESS

"I can conquer anything if I know others are depending on me."

BILL ROSENFIELD, NEW CASTLE, PA

R eader, the following success points are absolutely essential for
making a company, corporation, or international organization
profitable year after year. The notes and ideas presented come from
years of experience and countless around-the-world travels.

We (the authors) present these guide points because we have
lived them. We have had all the victories and difficulties a person

could experience in a lifetime. We have stumbled, fallen, gotten up, and kept going. We've dined with wealth and held the hand of poverty. We've gone to uncharted locations with only a one-way ticket and survived. We've met famous people, gentle people, and folks just trying to get by. We wrote this book so you'll know in your heart that you're never alone. You'll come to realize that anything is possible if you don't give up on your dreams or surrender to others who doubt. This world is a grand opportunity for possibilities, and we, as far as we know, only have one chance at life.

We all need to be the best we can be, never looking back, always making new acquaintances, exploring, asking questions. We should know, deep down inside, that we did our best, helped everyone we could, and never intentionally hurt anyone.

1. <u>Take care of and protect your employees:</u> Any company in the world is only as good as the people who work for it. Every day the master leader has to let his employees know they are genuinely appreciated and respected. All employees need to feel they are true members of a close-knit family that will always rally 'round in good times and bad. Employees have to know that they can depend on their leader, day or night, to vouch for them and come to their rescue if necessary. When everyone in the company feels secure and important, true success cannot be avoided. Leaders know without great employees who show dedication and loyalty every single day of the year, they would only be solitary souls wandering through life, chasing dreams and goals that never materialize. Without devoted employees, the leader has no one to share and understand his purpose and no one to support his visionary intentions. The leader needs his people, and they in turn need him. This is the miracle of harmoniously working together and respecting each other. When the leader teaches all he knows and encourages others to be greater than they ever imagined on their own, endless hope and spirit come alive, enveloping all. The leader will always stand up for his employees, care for his employees, and comfort them when everyone else has run away. In the course

of things, employees are the foundation for everything that progresses.

Nothing manmade can start, develop, or thrive without important people wanting to work, wanting challenges, and wanting to feel good about themselves. All leaders know this and give thanks every night for such wonderful employees and blessings.

2. Take care of your customers: Customer loyalty is what every company in the world strives for. Without dependable customers and their referrals, no organization can grow, much less survive. When a company's salesperson sells someone their product, their job is only half done. The other half (which most salespeople dislike because of details) involves taking care of the customer after the sale, making sure the customer stays satisfied and not forgotten. Only a fly-by-night company can afford (if that's the correct word) to sell its product and then abandon its customers. Valued customers (humans with wants and needs) are what keep any company going. The master leader knows it takes extra time and effort, but he should have people who write to customers on holidays and special dates important to the customer. The company should have personal calls made to give product updates or any other company information that might be of interest to the customer. Every person in the company should treat each and every customer as if their whole existence depended on them. Leaders understand when you treat a customer like they're worth a million dollars, they not only will come back to have their ego stroked, but they'll wind up buying more products.

Customers want to be treated special, like they are royalty. If a company makes each customer feel truly welcome and genuinely appreciated, then it's nearly impossible to keep the customer or customers from coming back. Just think for a minute, where else is a person going to go where everyone treats him like a big shot and people go out of their way to make him comfortable? All successful companies take extra care of their customers. It's not only a sound business practice, it's smart and the right thing to do. If a company takes their customers for granted, then the customer will do likewise, and in no time at all, what once was will not be remembered.

....

"Leadership is dependent on decisions, not time or acquaintances."

SAUL DURBIN, NEW YORK, NY

....

3. <u>Know your competition:</u> Any company that doesn't know its competition is doomed to fail. One of the most disastrous things that can happen to a corporation is for one of its rivals to suddenly and out of nowhere introduce to the public a similar and/or better product. There is no excuse for this kind of a business blunder. When a company is unexpectedly caught flat-footed by its competition, it's really too late to effectively react because the damage has already been done. Free trade and competition are the names of the game, and the more competitive one company is with another, the better for the consumer. Any corporation that refuses to compete or ignores customer demands by thinking it can survive on its past reputation is downright foolish.

Readers, if you look around, there are plenty of secure old giants that are now parking lots. Daily, the master leader will hawkishly keep up with any new and progressive trends in the marketplace. He'll go over reports, listen closely to chatter and whispers, and investigate any product development that might, in the future, affect his company. The leader understands the harder he tries to improve his company, the harder the competition will try to keep up. The business world is a fascinating place to learn, grow, and prosper. But, if a person or company becomes complacent, thinking their glory days will never end, then all they for a change of heart is sit down, look around, and breathe the dust of spirited others who unapologetically passed them by.

If a company expects to remain successful, it should never stoop to throwing putdowns or bad-mouthing the competition. No one company comes out a winner when firms downgrade each other. When a company abides by honest principles, improves its products, keeps competitive, and resists dirty politics, then the public will invariably gravitate towards it, and, in the long run, everyone benefits.

"The spirits of the young protect others from fear and memories sprinkled with regret."

LINDA COSTANZO, ALBUQUERQUE, NM

---

4. <u>Get young people working in the company:</u> For any company to survive and prosper, it has to get new blood into its system. If a company depends on only its good old pros or good old days techniques, then it will die a slow, painful, and well-deserved death. The master leader knows that bright and enthusiastic young people have the courage and daring to try new things, invent new paradigms, and challenge everything. Young, aggressive employees are the heartbeat of tomorrow. These folks will connect the future dots. Young and energetic employees enrich everyone they come in contact with. They are an enterprise within themselves. They create ideas, thoughts, and new ventures never before dreamed of. Young employees with their drive and can-do attitude are power sources for any and all progress. These wonderful talents, with their imaginative plans and sense of adventure, are valuable intangibles no company can do without.

The leader mixes the young folks with the older folks so both can grow, learn, and share. The leader realizes that "Today" is "Tomorrow" early, and he makes his plans on the gifts given to younger spirits. The leader needs boldness supporting his undertakings, and he needs advice that is innocent and clear, not reserved or tainted. So many times in business, the factor of innocence shames the practice of rigid and conventional behavior. Young people are the hope of tomorrow, and any company that refuses to acknowledge that is, as stated before, sentenced to ruin.

One last note to remember: the young at heart can be found in all ages. What matters is attitude, and when one's outlook is of promise and fascination, then any age rules chiseled in stone should be thrown out the window.

5. <u>Don't tell all your secrets:</u> The master leader can keep secrets. Period. If the leader wants his company to be around for a long time, he will faithfully practice the basic business code of not revealing sensitive information to others. If a lot of company personnel are privy to everything the leader does or does not do, then many areas of the company's endeavors could very well be in jeopardy. All successful corporations conduct their private business behind closed doors. As everyone knows, the business world is full of copycats who will steal a company's ideas or marketing campaign in a second.

Secrecy is vital when operating a competitive enterprise, and secrecy is a key factor that can bond employees together into a tighter and stronger unit. For example, within a company, if a few select people are chosen to know a secret plan that will be used to promote the company's product, that secret shared in trust and loyalty will be a grand catalyst that unites and empowers. This secret will make the chosen employees feel important, thus creating closeness to the company that could not be manufactured any other way. The leader also has an obligation to his employees when it comes to secrets. He must never disclose private information people have shared with him. Employees will forever work with and defend a leader they know they can trust and depend on.

Secrecy is an intricate part of business conversations and negotiations for all leaders, and must be managed with care. They are as flammable or as harmless as their contents, and typically carry little or no value. The leader never abuses their position or scars their self-respect by betraying those who talked to him in secret.

"I depend on mistakes to direct, strengthen, and to keep me humble all at the same time."

ANDREW HUDSON, MARIETTA, GA

6. <u>Learn from past mistakes:</u> All leaders know any company in the world that doesn't learn from past mistakes is destined to repeat them. Mistakes and missteps are just a part of life, but they are also important experiences that teach and direct. If a company or its master leader fails to immediately correct or address mistakes, then any extra time and energy used for mistake examination, deliberation, and head scratching will, in the long run, cost money. When a mistake is made, get it taken care of and make sure it doesn't happen again! Period. Live and learn have been the growing ingredients for mankind forever, and this process will always be with us. But, be wise and intelligent; attack any problem head-on so it's over and done with. Don't dwell on mistakes and think, "What if?" Put them where they belong: in a buried box with a tombstone that reads, "Never again."

7. <u>Get advice:</u> When the master leader doesn't know exactly how to deal with a certain problem or situation that develops in his company, then he will, without any fanfare or public announcement, seek outside advice. It doesn't matter whether the trouble is legal or financial; outside and independent viewpoints and guidance should always be welcome. There will be many times in the leader's career when he feels that some subject or circumstance is over his head; that is when he wisely asks for help. If he, because of his pride, tries to remedy the situation on his own, he could very easily be courting disaster. Always ask others who have experienced the same or similar dilemmas what they did to overcome the problem. Remember, no one has all the answers and no one is perfect.

8. <u>Advertise:</u> If a company doesn't advertise its product, then its competition will bury it alive. It simply takes money to make

money, and there is no way to get around this business fact. No matter what kind of technological system or prevailing communication method a company uses, the public has to know about the company's product before they can purchase the product. The secret to successful advertising can be summed up in seven words: "Get the public's attention and keep it." If a company can, through all of today's avant-garde outlets, initially catch the public's imagination and interest, then in time, customers will appear. Product loyalties will develop, and the company that advertises will enjoy its rightful share in its particular marketplace.

Master leaders also know that word of mouth is a very important means of advertising. They understand that one satisfied customer will tell only two or three people about their good purchase, but a customer who is upset with a company or product will tell eight to ten others.

....

"Working without reliable records is like having a compass without a needle."

DAVID VAUGHN SR., ST. PAUL, MN

....

9. <u>Keep good records:</u> All successful companies keep exact, detailed, daily records on every bit of business done. The company needs to record all financial transactions (for tax purposes) and log up-to-date data that shows overall sales volume, closing percentage, and any other information reflecting progress, manufacturing, logistics, transportation, and production. The master leader requires these vital reports to run the business effectively every minute of the day. Legitimate figures, documents, and files help keep him informed. The leader will also chart and record any and all developments involving product improvement or alterations. Don't forget, reader, when all company information is safeguarded with backup systems and other security measures, everyone associated with the company sleeps better.

10. <u>Have fun:</u> The master leader understands that if his employees aren't happy but are always worried, stressed out, too serious, and don't allow themselves any time for a little fun, then his office is not going to be very successful. The truth is, any group of unhappy employees can't spread enthusiasm and good will to customers. Coach Frank Broyles of the University of Arkansas said, "Take pride in your work, prove yourself on every play, have dedication, have a good time, and the score will take care of itself." This kind of positive outlook and attitude needs to be kept alive in any company, organization, or corporation. Employees can create more, imagine bigger, develop deeper, and perform better when a sense of fun and respectable team spirit permeates the office. Having fun in the workplace and looking forward to daily challenges are the intangible byproducts of self-confidence and laughter. Employees want to be happy about coming to work. They don't want to walk in the door of their company with their head down, dreading the work ahead of them, and not knowing if they'll even be there the next day. That is why the master leader is not only the head businessman or woman. He is the cheerleader for all his people, letting them know they are important, they are needed, and that it's alright to laugh and have fun because it's contagious. And who wouldn't want to be around smiles and good times?

"The more you lead, the stronger you'll get, and the stronger you get, the more you'll be needed."

UNKNOWN

Conclusion

CONCLUSION

At the end of the day, it all boils down to this: master leaders are successful because they make their employees successful. They engage, empower, and respect each and every person they employ. Period. Effective leaders always acknowledge and encourage from the bottom up, not the top down. For any company to have continued success or have positive turnarounds occur, the leader will first establish a trust with the employees who make up the foundation of a company. These special souls, day in and day out, do their jobs with pride and dedication. All progress and prosperity depend upon these employees' shoulders. The leader will, in their wisdom, always take the time to thank and care for these people, teach and advise. All the while, they never forget the secret of greatness, "When you put another person first, you will never be last."

The leader stands with conviction in front of their employees, not behind closed doors. They cheer and reprimand when necessary with love and understanding in their heart. They guide, question, and are always curious about people. The leader takes the time to deliver handwritten notes to the employees, knowing that in today's business world the use of convenient technology systems to communicate won't ever compare to a personal, signed message that cannot be discarded or forgotten. Master leaders don't push; they pull, they reward. They try not to disappoint, embracing the power of humility and integrity—a very difficult but possible ambition that challenges leaders every single day.

Master leaders inspire their employees to love themselves, to chase rainbows, face disappointment, and fight for their beliefs. Leaders realize that they can't please everyone. They know success doesn't depend on fancy words or carrots. They understand employees want hands-on examples, not charts or diagrams that show or promote discussion.

Employees, no matter what their responsibility, want leaders who appreciate their personalities and desires. They expect fair and honest decisions, firm action, and loyalty. When people have a leader they can talk to, without fear of being ridiculed or taken for granted, then there is nothing in the world that can stop or impede their performance.

Great leaders have a great accountability clause in their contract with their employees. This clause is not set it stone, but in spirit. It states in brief, "If my people fail, it's because I failed them. If my people are victorious, I hope I helped. If my people abandon me, it's because I ignored them, and if we all meet on the plains of success, agreeing we made it together, then I can walk away knowing I'll never be alone."

Remember, reader, you can only lead others if they believe in you…and you can only get others to believe in you if you truly believe in yourself.

THE END

About the Authors

James W. White is a well-versed, respected, passionate and dynamic sales leader who delivers continued success across all venues while championing countless people to new heights in both their personal and professional lives. With a diverse background that includes the United States Navy, owning his own insurance and investment planning business, real estate sales, executive consulting, and leading $200+ million sales teams within the resort industry, his ability to win in all economic climates remains resolute.

As a graduate of the esteemed Linkage Leadership Academy and Wharton's School of Business Global Leadership program, his leadership disposition, business acumen, and ability to surpass all goals through positive and impactful influence speaks for itself. Additionally, Jim serves on the Executive Advisory Board for the College of Business, UNLV, and is an active leader in their Global Entrepreneur Scholarship program.

James was born in West Covina, California, raised in Flagstaff, Arizona, and attended Northern Arizona University. He currently resides in Las Vegas, Nevada, with his wife of sixteen years, his son, and daughter.

James W. Pickens is one of the most dynamic and respected sales educators in the world. He and his work have been featured in *Publisher's Weekly*, *Wall Street Journal*, and *Success* magazine. His audio books are in-flight on American Airlines, and he has been featured on countless talk shows around the world.

Pickens was born in New Orleans and educated at the University of Arkansas and the University of Colorado. After serving in Vietnam, he formed his own business, becoming a multi-millionaire by the age of thirty-seven. Pickens is the author of *The Art of Closing Any Deal*, *The Closers*, *More Art of Closing Any Deal*, *Cleopatra's Secrets of Negotiations and Persuasion for Women*, and *The One Minute Closer*. Combined, these books have sold several million copies worldwide. Pickens is on the executive board of advisors, College of Business, at the University of Nevada, Las Vegas (UNLV).

Mr. Pickens has one daughter and two grandsons, and he resides in Dallas, Texas, and Prescott, Arizona.